THE FIRST FLIGHT

THE FIRST FLIGHT

The Origins of the New Zealand Bomber Squadron

Chris Newey

www.aviationbooks.org

First published 2024 by Aviation Books Ltd., Merthyr Tydfil, CF47 8RY, United Kingdom

Publisher's email address for correspondence: aviationbooksuk@gmail.com

Copyright 2024 © Chris Newey

The right of Chris Newey to be identified as Author of this work is asserted by him in accordance with the Copyright, Designs and Patents Act 1988.

All rights reserved. No part of this publication may be reproduced, stored in a retrieval system, transmitted in any form or by any means, electronic, mechanical, or photocopied, recorded or otherwise, without the written permission of the copyright owners.

Editor: Andy Wright, Wright Stuff Editing & Proofreading.

Cover design: Topics – The Creative Partnership www.topicsdesign.co.uk

Photographs and other illustrations of these incidents are available on the internet, but it is difficult in most cases to establish their original source, especially as a large number of photographs appear on numerous different websites. The author has sought permission to use the images in every case, although this has not been possible in all, due to broken links on old websites, or publishers having gone out of business. Where the source is clear, but no answer has been forthcoming, the author has assessed the historical value of each picture when deciding whether or not to include it. By definition, every contemporary image used is more than one hundred years old, and the advice received is that their use is permissible under copyright law. This has been carried out in good faith.

Any queries or objections to the use of any images or other material should be referred to the publisher.

A CIP catalogue reference for this book is available from the British Library.

ISBN 9781915335494

Cover image: Air to air view of New Zealand Squadron Wellington I NZ302, flying from RAF Station Harwell, November 1939 - Air Force Museum of New Zealand, ref 2017.171.07

Colourisation: Nathan Howland - HowdiColour Recovery and Colour

Contents

Introduction 7
Building an Air Force 9
Bringing the Bombers Back 23
The Wellingtons 31
The New Zealand Squadron 41
Preparations Back Home 48
The 1st Mobile Flight 53
War Intervenes 67
Taking Stock 71
Nobody's Children 77
Building a Squadron 83
The First Operations 88
Seal of Approval 93
First Blood 104
A New Fighting Force 119
Postscripts 124
Buck's Treasure 133
Sources 135
Acknowledgements 138
Appendices 139
    New Zealand Squadron personnel, May 1939 – 4 April 1940 140
    List of 1st Mobile Flight personnel 160
    List of 2nd–4th Mobile Flights personnel 162
    The NZ Wellingtons 165
Index 173

Introduction

Return At Dawn by Charles Cundall ARA

Hanging on the wall in the Officers Mess at RNZAF Base Ohakea is a painting called *Return at Dawn* by English painter Charles Cundall. It shows airmen on a wartime bomber station in England welcoming a Wellington crew back from a night operation over Europe in July 1940.

The pilot, in distinctive white overalls, is met by his wing commander, while his crew emerge from the aircraft and two more Wellingtons circle overhead in a vast dawn sky, waiting to land. The scene is beautifully lit with the soft glow of a new day.

The men and aircraft belong to No. 75 New Zealand Squadron, the first Commonwealth squadron to be formed in the Royal Air Force (RAF) during the Second World War and the only New Zealand heavy bomber squadron in the RAF.

The 'New Zealand Bomber Squadron' became famous for its many accomplishments – and a source of great national pride – in particular, the Victoria Cross earned by Sergeant 'Jimmy' Ward one memorable night in July 1941. The squadron's daring exploits were reported on regularly in wartime newspapers and later written up for consumption in New Zealand, firstly by author Hilary St. George Saunders in a 1942 publication also titled *Return at Dawn*, then in 1945 by war correspondent Alan W. Mitchell in *New Zealanders in the Air War*.

Three squadron histories have been written: Norman Franks's *Forever Strong* published in 1991; an unpublished history compiled over many years by members of the New Zealand 75 Squadron

Association; and *75 (NZ) Squadron* from Chris Ward's 'Bomber Command Squadron Profiles' series, initially published in 2018.

However, the story of how a New Zealand bomber squadron came about in the first place has never been properly told, the details overshadowed by subsequent momentous events and often brushed over in official accounts. This book is an attempt to tell that story. It involves one of the RAF's most respected leaders, the architect of the wartime Royal New Zealand Air Force.

A crucial part of his plan to reorganise New Zealand's almost non-existent air defences in the late 1930s was to purchase 30 new bomber aircraft. But the bombers were built in England and had to be delivered halfway around the world, something never attempted before.

The pilot and the wing commander in Cundall's painting played key roles. They led a small team, which included some of New Zealand's most skilled and experienced pilots, in detailed planning and intensive training for a series of bold long-distance ferry flights.

Back home, new aerodromes had to be built specifically to house the new bombers, Ohakea on the North Island being one of them.

War intervened and the pioneering ferry flights were cancelled.

The group stayed on in England and, in the end, made history of a different kind.

Building an Air Force

In October 1933, when Germany dramatically and unexpectedly pulled out of the World Disarmament Conference, Hitler dissolved the Reichstag, called for new elections and claimed the right of Germany to equality in armaments. Germany then pulled out of the League of Nations and, by 1934, it was clear to the rest of the world Hitler was re-arming.

Britain was forced to recognise the dream of world peace was now unrealistic and announced a major expansion of the Royal Air Force (RAF). With Japan becoming increasingly aggressive, New Zealand also began to feel vulnerable.

Michael Savage's first Labour government came to power in November 1935, bringing a new brand of socialist politics and a new wave of radical reform. However, even this idealistic group of evangelicals, pacifists and trade unionists could not ignore the international situation.

Prime Minister Savage was a critic of Britain's appeasement policies towards Italy, Japan, Spain and Germany, and a strong supporter of the League of Nations. Britain had given multiple assurances it would commit to the defence of Australia and New Zealand, in the event of an attack by Japan, by sending its fleet to Singapore where a major naval base was under construction. But the promises were less than convincing; Britain was now facing threats in Europe and it was obvious the fleet could not be in two places at once. The new government quickly grasped the implications.

Developments in aviation had convinced several of Savage's team that air defence was going to be a more cost-effective and flexible way of meeting potential offshore threats. However, the tiny organisation that constituted the country's air force had never been properly resourced since the Great War and had struggled through the Depression under the control of the General Officer Commanding New Zealand Military Forces.

In 1920, New Zealand had been offered a gift of 100 war-surplus aircraft by Britain to encourage development of air defence, and to help ensure compatibility of equipment with the RAF. Unbelievably, the government prevaricated, concerned about the cost of maintaining such a fleet, and eventually accepted just 33 aircraft. Instead of building an air force around these, however, six were kept for military use and the rest were loaned or leased to commercial operators.

The loan/lease aircraft were enthusiastically taken up by entrepreneurs; commercial aviation began to grow in New Zealand while military aviation languished. New Zealand's 'air force' consisted of Captain Len Isitt and a staff of three operating out of the Sockburn (Christchurch) premises of the Canterbury Aviation Company (CAC).

The government did, however, agree to subsidise annual refresher courses for former Royal Flying Corps, Royal Naval Air Service and RAF pilots – privately run by CAC at Sockburn and the New Zealand Flying School at Kohimarama in Auckland – to help maintain a reserve of flying officers. The first of these courses took place at Sockburn in January–March 1923.

In June 1923, the New Zealand Permanent Air Force (NZPAF) was formed (as part of the Permanent Forces) alongside the New Zealand Air Force (NZAF, part of the Territorial Forces). That same year, largely due to the foresight and generosity of CAC's Sir Henry Wigram, the government acquired Sockburn as its first military airfield, immediately renaming it Wigram in his honour.

In 1924, the NZPAF took over the refresher courses. The second edition was held at Wigram for the 72 officers of the newly formalised Air Force Reserve, the pilots who would form the nucleus of the NZAF.

Work started on a second aerodrome (and seaplane base) at Hobsonville near Auckland in 1927 and, in 1930, the NZPAF undertook its first active operations in Samoa.

In 1934, the NZPAF was renamed the Royal New Zealand Air Force, a title considered rather grandiose by the press of the day, with an establishment of only nine officers and 49 other ranks.

An order had been placed in 1933 for eight Vickers Vildebeest biplanes (later increased to 12), originally designed as torpedo bombers, to be used by the RNZAF as reconnaissance bombers. Despite the British Air Ministry's enthusiasm for New Zealand's air force expansion, the reality was the RAF's own expansion and production priorities meant the first of the Vildebeests did not arrive until April 1935. Furthermore, as the newspapers were quick to point out, they came with neither torpedoes nor bombs.

Four Avro 626 advanced trainers were also purchased, to add to the four Hawker Tomtit trainers, two Fairey IIIF seaplanes, one Saro Cutty Sark flying boat and a handful of obsolete Bristol Fighters, Gloster Grebes and de Havilland Moths.

As of 31 May 1936, the RNZAF consisted of 20 officers and 107 other ranks, with 74 NZAF officers in reserve.[1]

This was the RNZAF Savage's Labour government had inherited.

The government felt, with limited funds, expansion of New Zealand's air defences would be the most cost-effective path. But the British Chiefs of Staff disagreed, insisting the maintenance of two Royal Navy cruisers on the New Zealand Station would be more effective. Imperial Defence policy viewed the pivotal Singapore naval base as key to the defence of the Pacific and looked to New Zealand to support and contribute to that.

New Zealand was justifiably sceptical of the policy. It had already contributed £1 million towards the Singapore base, only to have Britain postpone work on it. The expectation was that, in the event of a threat to Singapore, New Zealand's two cruisers would immediately be sent to assist, leaving the country defenceless.

As urged by various experts, it was finally agreed the RNZAF should be reorganised, properly resourced and made into an independent service. Squadron Leader Tom Wilkes, Director of Air Services, was given the job of coming up with a plan and working out the costs. He felt that, for such an expensive and important exercise, an experienced independent view was needed.

A request was sent to Britain and Wing Commander Ralph Alexander Cochrane AFC RAF, on loan from the U.K. Air Ministry, was sent out to New Zealand.

A 41-year-old Scot, a tireless worker and 'a very brainy chap', according to a fellow RAF officer,[2] Cochrane had joined the Royal Navy in 1912 and served during the First World War as an airship pilot in the Royal Naval Air Service (RNAS), then as a test pilot and staff officer in the Admiralty's Airship Department, helping develop new airship designs and mooring masts.[3] It was in this role that he became friends with a young draughtsman working for Vickers on rigid airship design – Barnes Wallis.

In 1919, Cochrane was awarded an Air Force Cross for his test pilot work, granted a permanent commission in the RAF and posted to Air HQ Middle East in Egypt. His job entailed testing airship fabrics and finding a suitable site for a station to be part of a proposed Imperial airship route to Australia and New Zealand. However, in 1921, he received a valuable piece of advice from none other than Air Marshal Sir Hugh Trenchard – the father of the RAF – who was visiting on an inspection of local RAF units: 'Young man, you are wasting your time, go and learn to fly an aeroplane.'

Cochrane took heed and trained as an aeroplane pilot. His next posting was to Iraq with No. 45 (Bomber) Squadron flying Vickers Vernons and serving as a flight commander under Squadron Leader Arthur

'Bert' Harris and alongside Flight Lieutenant Robert Saundby, both of whom would play important roles in his later career.

In 1924, Cochrane took up a position at the RAF's Cranwell training establishment. In 1925, he attended RAF Staff College, Andover, graduating the following year and, now promoted to squadron leader, took up a training role at HQ Wessex Bombing Area. During this period, he reconnected with Arthur Harris at No. 58 Squadron and got to know another future mentor, Wing Commander Charles Portal.

In 1928, he was posted to HQ Aden Command, then served as commander of No. 8 Squadron at RAF Khormaksar, operating Fairey IIIF bombers.

In 1929, he took up an appointment at the RAF Staff College, subsequently joining the Directorate of the Chief of the Air Staff in the Department of Operations and Intelligence.

In 1935, he attended the Imperial Defence College, where he studied the threats posed by Germany and Japan and was then appointed to the headquarters of Inland Area and Training Command.

It was in fact Arthur Harris, now at the Air Ministry, who rang Cochrane to ask him if he would like to go out to New Zealand. The job was expected to take about four months.

It was the third time New Zealand had requested advice from Britain on its air defences. Both previous reports had been submitted by senior RAF officers – Colonel Arthur Bettington in 1919 and Air Marshall Sir John Salmond in 1928. Both reports detailed the critical role of an air force in defending New Zealand from seaborne attack and, in both cases, major elements were rejected by the governments of the day due to cost. Probably for this reason, the Air Ministry decided to send a less senior officer this time, albeit one who was very well regarded. And, this time, the New Zealand Government could ill afford to ignore the expertise and advice offered.

Cochrane accepted and was briefed by the Air Ministry. Not that he needed convincing, but current British air defence thinking gave pre-eminence to the bomber, as promoted by Trenchard and articulated in Prime Minister Baldwin's hopeful statement, 'The bomber always gets through …'

The Air Ministry saw an opportunity to standardise New Zealand's air defences with the RAF and to effectively extend imperial air power. The Dominions were expected to assist in protecting the Empire's trade routes in the Pacific and Far East, as well as help strengthen the Singapore base, contributing material and manpower. These aspects would have to be considered, not just New Zealand's local defence needs.

Cochrane left England on the ocean liner RMS *Mataroa* on 2 October 1936. He worked on his report during the voyage:

> The report was easy and was based on a good map and certain assumptions about the possible scale of attack which the Air Ministry had given me.[4]

In his downtime, he socialised with the other passengers and read Margaret Mitchell's new novel *Gone With The Wind*. He had the bulk of the report written by the time he disembarked at Auckland on Saturday 7 November.

In his first interview with the New Zealand press that afternoon, Cochrane outlined the issues he would need to address and, while discussing his recent experiences in training and expansion, mentioned the potential to entice back the more than 100 New Zealand pilots already serving in the RAF.

RNZAF line-up at Wigram, circa 1936: five Vickers Vildebeests, two Avro 626s, four Hawker Tomtits and one Gloster Grebe. (James Lloyd Findlay personal album collection, 1983-272.49, Air Force Museum of NZ)

The next morning, Cochrane inspected Auckland's Hobsonville aerodrome with the station's commanding officer, Squadron Leader Len Isitt. He left Auckland on the 'Night Limited' express on the Sunday evening, arriving in Wellington on Monday morning.

His first meeting was with Minister of Defence Fred Jones, General Officer Commanding New Zealand Military Forces Major-General Sinclair-Burgess and Director of Air Services Tom Wilkes. His working relationships with Jones and Wilkes would be critical; fortunately, both were supportive and open to his ideas.

He met with Prime Minister Savage and key members of the government including Walter Nash (Finance), Peter Fraser (Health and Education), Bob Semple (Public Works) and the aviation-minded John A. Lee. Cochrane also established an immediate friendship with Governor-General Viscount Galway. He received strong support from senior RNZAF officers, particularly Len Isitt and Arthur Nevill, and found a friend and ally in Esmond Gibson, a civil engineer, head of the Aerodrome Services Branch of the New Zealand Public Works Department (PWD), adviser to Wilkes, and a flight lieutenant in the Territorial Air Force.

By the 20th, Cochrane had finished his first draft of the report and shared it with Captain Robert Oliver RN for comment.[5] Oliver was the 2nd Member of the Naval Board, Cochrane's approximate naval equivalent, and his opinion would have been valued. The plan represented a major shift in the country's defence priorities in favour of air. Next, he shared it with Wilkes. He did not want to show it to Jones yet, preferring the government ministers read the report in its entirety.

Both Oliver and Wilkes were supportive of the plan, so Cochrane set about tidying the proof and writing a summary to finish it off. After two days, and suffering from a bad head cold, he wrote:

> I felt too muzzy to read it so sent it back and told them to go ahead. If I read the BEASTLY THING again I am bound to want to make more alterations.

Within three weeks of arriving in the country, Cochrane had finalised his report. He sent it off to the Government Printer on 23 November.

Cochrane had been corresponding with his friend Barnes Wallis. After airship development had been abandoned, Wallis had been moved into the Vickers Aviation design team to work under Rex Pierson, the chief aircraft designer. Wallis had developed a 'geodetic' airframe structure – a lightweight latticework spaceframe of great strength – inspired by his previous work on airships. It had first been employed in the Vickers Wellesley light bomber, but Pierson and Wallis were now working on a larger twin-engine bomber of similar construction to meet Air Ministry specification B.9/32. The Vickers Type 271 prototype made its first flight on 15 June 1936; this was the bomber Cochrane had in mind for the RNZAF:

> Wrote to ... Wallis about the B 9/32. Aerodromes are so small that it is necessary to be certain that aircraft can use them without risk.

Interestingly, in his own report the previous year, Wilkes had foreseen the need for bombers with trans-Tasman capability and urged investigation of 'the new multi-engined machine of geodetic design'.[6] It was the same aircraft Cochrane was now recommending – the aircraft that would come to be known as the Vickers Wellington.

On the 28th, Cochrane took the overnight inter-island ferry *Maori* to Lyttelton, to make his first visit to Wigram. Accompanied by 'Gibby' Gibson, he was generally impressed with Squadron Leader Jim Findlay and his staff but frustrated by what he described as 'penny-wise stupidities' in the aerodrome facilities and administration.

While in Christchurch, he stayed with Air Marshal Sir Robert and Lady Clark-Hall. Clark-Hall had been a squadron and wing commander in the RNAS during the First World War, then a senior commander in the RAF, retiring to New Zealand in 1934. He was a perfect sounding board for Cochrane's ideas:

> His only doubts as to whether N.Z. would not be better off with all air & no navy; but after C.O.S. telegram this is not (a) solution I can sponsor.

Cochrane left Christchurch on 2 December to return to Wellington.

He presented his 'Report on the air aspect of the defence problems of New Zealand, including the suggested duties, strength and organization of the New Zealand Air Force' to Fred Jones, Minister Defence, on Friday 4 December, outlining a plan for a major expansion and reorganisation of the service.[7]

A key element of Cochrane's plan was the acquisition of a long-range reconnaissance and strike capability that could reach Australia, the Pacific Islands and, if necessary, Singapore. The longest leg involved, Darwin–Singapore, was 1,700 miles. The main threat to New Zealand was seen as seaborne attack, so his recommendation was for two squadrons of medium bombers, land planes not flying boats, capable of locating and attacking enemy units before they reached the New Zealand coast:

> To sum up:
>
> The defence requirements appear to call for a long-range multi-engine aircraft; and these requirements can be met by the type known as the medium bomber which is now being put into production for the Royal Air Force. This is estimated to carry 2 tons of bombs, 1,000 miles cruising at 200 miles per hour, whilst with a lesser bomb load and slightly slower speed the distance can be increased to 2,000 miles.
>
> Taking into account the area over which operations may extend, it is recommended that the Royal New Zealand Air Force should consist of not less than two squadrons having a total first-line strength of twenty-four aircraft, and with adequate base facilities and reserves.
>
> It would be desirable for these two squadrons to be stationed on the same aerodrome in order to economise in base equipment and to simplify control, and the most suitable location would be Auckland.

Considering airborne attack unlikely, Cochrane discounted fighters from his plan and instead recommended a supporting Army co-operation squadron of smaller aircraft.

He calculated the flying personnel required to maintain two bomber squadrons and one Army co-operation squadron under wartime conditions as 250 pilots, 125 wireless operators and 125 air gunners. To achieve that, an RNZAF training school would be established at Wigram; aero clubs would provide elementary pilot training.

The plan came with a substantial shopping list: a new permanent RNZAF station would need to be built for the two bomber squadrons; the bombers themselves with associated equipment (plus 25% reserve), bombs and bomb storage; additions to Wigram for the new flying school; expansion of Hobsonville for stores and maintenance; new training aircraft; construction of landing grounds in the Pacific; and development of wireless communications. Cochrane estimated the total cost to come to £1,124,000 sterling. He went on to recommend the Air Force operate as a separate service controlled by an Air Board under the Minister of Defence.

Cochrane met with the minister the following day, pleasantly surprised that Jones already had a good grasp of the issues:

> He thought the capital cost might be too high, but on the whole was favourable, although obviously the scope of operations which I had advocated went beyond anything which he had contemplated.

The Cabinet met at 10:00am on 8 December to consider the report and, after a few questions to Cochrane, approved it in full. The government was so pleased with Cochrane's work that they invited him to stay on for another two years to help implement the plan. He accepted, subject to approval by the Air Ministry, and a formal offer was made on 17 December.

Without further consultation with Britain, and without releasing any details to the public, Savage's government immediately began to put Cochrane's report into action, not even waiting for the appropriate legislation to be drawn up.[8]

On the 18th, Cochrane and Gibson drove to Palmerston North to look at potential aerodrome sites around Ohakea. From there, Cochrane began his summer holiday break as guest of Thomas Hislop, the Mayor of Wellington. They headed north to Tongariro and Taupo for the trout fishing, then up to Rotorua on Christmas Day. There he fished, golfed, played tourist, socialised and met up with the famous New Zealand aviator Jean Batten, who had completed the first solo flight from England to New Zealand only three months before.

On Monday 4 January 1937, holiday over, Cochrane was flown to Auckland, via Tauranga and Thames, by Flight Lieutenant Maurice Buckley. It was Cochrane's first flight in an RNZAF aircraft, a de Havilland Moth; although he could not know it at the time, his pilot would one day play a major part in his grand plan.

In Auckland, Cochrane and Gibson inspected more potential bomber aerodrome sites west of Hobsonville and around Kumeu, with Gibson starting a proper survey on the 16th. Cochrane returned to Wellington and, with Isitt and Nevill added to his team, and his RAF station plans recently arrived from England, began the huge job of rebuilding the Air Force.

One of his first decisions was whether to organise his bomber force around one station or two. His initial preference for a cost-effective single Auckland station was soon overtaken by strategic considerations and the plan was modified to build two stations – one central, one northern.

Coincidentally, Harold Gatty, Australian aviator and Pan American Airways representative, happened to be in hospital in Wellington and the two had several very useful discussions on Pacific air routes, which were also within Cochrane's purview. This was a politically sensitive subject as the British had their own plans for the Pacific and were hoping to head off the Americans. Much to London's annoyance, the New Zealand Government had already signed an agreement with Pan American; Gatty was in New Zealand to prepare for an initial survey flight. The strategic importance of the Pacific islands was inextricably intertwined with the development of commercial air routes and access to landing grounds.

Cochrane put forward a plan for a network of four reconnaissance routes radiating out from Fiji, with surveys and plans required to have facilities ready by the time the Wellingtons arrived.[9] The suggested routes 'would enable aircraft to reach the greater part of the South Pacific if the need arose'.

The Royal New Zealand Air Force was established as an independent service on 1 April 1937, under the control of the new Air Department; Cochrane was appointed Chief of the Air Staff. In August, his promotion to group captain came through from London.

That month, the first details of his plan were made public when newspapers reported[10] the government was to purchase Britain's latest and most-advanced bomber, the Wellington, a type so new that to date only one prototype had flown:

> The third type to be purchased is the Vickers Wellington, a long range, twin-engined, mid-wing monoplane with a long wingspan and capable of travelling at great heights. Its range remains a secret, but it could easily hop the Tasman Sea. It falls into the heavy-bomber class, has a speed of over 200 m.p.h., and possesses a sting in its tail. It is altogether a formidable machine and one which will make air co-operation with Australia, or even of the Singapore Base, something within the ability of this country.

The reports also addressed the infrastructure required for the new aircraft:

> Ground organisation is being planned under the direction of a special officer who recently arrived on loan from the British Air Ministry. One aspect of the new ground organisation is the development of the centrally situated aerodrome at Ohakea, near Palmerston North, as a central base for the North Island, with a possible additional field at Auckland and extensions at Wigram to meet the new needs there.

The central site needed to be out of range of attack from the sea, but with favourable weather conditions and away from mountains.

In 1927, the Imperial Airship Communications Committee had visited New Zealand to identify potential sites for a commercial airship station as part of the British Government's Imperial Airship Scheme to form an air service between Britain and its Dominions.[11] The committee recommended a site, between the central North Island towns of Bulls and Sanson, named Ohakea. The airship scheme had been abandoned after the fatal crash of R.101 in France on 5 October 1930, but the landing site's advantages were still relevant.

Cochrane and Gibson had visited Ohakea in December 1936 and, in June 1937, after surveys had been completed, 486 acres of land were purchased. Construction started in February 1938.

The existing aerodrome at Hobsonville had been assessed as too small and, after some searching, a site for a possible new northern station was found at nearby Whenuapai.

In December 1937, air power's reach and the strategic value of Pacific air routes were emphasised when Pan American Airways' Sikorsky S-42 flying boat *Samoan Clipper* flew into Auckland from San Francisco via Pago Pago, and Imperial Airways' Short Empire flying boat *Centaurus* arrived the next day from England, via Sydney. The competition in aviation technology was accompanied by an undignified scramble to assert sovereignty over various strategic small islands along the key routes.

Back in March, during the Sikorsky's first visit to Auckland, Cochrane had been on board as a VIP guest on a goodwill flight to Napier and return. On 3 January, he was a VIP guest on *Centaurus* on a three-day trip from Wellington to Dunedin, via Lyttelton, and return.

Meanwhile, he had been working on the legislation required for his new air force and the establishment of an Air Board along the lines of the British Air Ministry. He was also working on expanding training and the revival of the four Territorial squadrons. In March 1938, 12 ex-Fleet Air Arm Blackburn Baffin torpedo bombers arrived for No. 2 (Wellington) Territorial Squadron, the first delivery out of 29 purchased.

At the same time, Cochrane and (now Squadron Leader) Gibson were overseeing the designs of the new RNZAF stations, working from the RAF plans.

Group Captain Ralph Alexander Cochrane AFC RAF at Rongotai, 4 June 1938. (ALB862456022, Air Force Museum of NZ)

Lord Galway and Group Captain Ralph Cochrane inspect RNZAF aircraft on display at Rongotai, 4 June 1938. They are accompanied by Lieutenant Lombard-Hobson RN ADC and Squadron Leader Arthur Nevill RNZAF. A Blackburn Baffin looms behind. (Air Force Museum of New Zealand)

In May, more details of Cochrane's plan were announced when Minister for Defence Fred Jones confirmed to the public that the government had placed an order (the previous year) for 30 new Vickers Wellington bombers at a total cost of £750,000:[12]

> The Wellington aircraft is the latest type to go into production and has a great range and load-carrying capacity. The aircraft will be flown to New Zealand as soon as the stations are ready to receive them.
>
> Orders have been placed for the immediate supply of ammunition for bombers, also for spare parts for machines and other spares.

Jones also confirmed the building of the two new operational stations as bases for the new bombers, at Ohakea and at Whenuapai, where 600 acres would be purchased the following month. Of direct relevance to the bomber capability, Jones announced an order had also been placed for five Airspeed Oxfords to serve as multi-engine trainers for the new pilot flying training school at Wigram.

Just a month later, on 4 June, the RNZAF held its first air display at Rongotai, Wellington, a Hendon-like military demonstration of expertise and an opportunity to show off the growing fleet of aircraft to the public. The large party of VIPs attending included Prime Minister Savage, Minister of Defence Jones and Governor-General Lord Galway, who inspected the airmen and machines with Cochrane.

One of the futuristic new Wellington bombers featured on the cover of the souvenir air show programme.

Souvenir programme, RNZAF Display, Rongotai, 4 June 1938. (Air Force Museum of NZ)

The Czech crisis of September 1938, along with the discovery Germany was planning raids down into the Pacific, led to a new review of the strategic situation by the Chiefs of Staff. Fiji, Tonga, the New Hebrides and New Caledonia, all possessing excellent harbours, were seen as particular threats to New Zealand if taken by Japan.[9]

The paper backed Cochrane's plan to prepare for deployment of the Wellingtons to the Pacific islands and for a survey be made of potential airfields, reconnaissance routes and lines of reinforcement. Fiji, in particular, was seen as critical, representing a potential base from which modern land-based bombers could attack New Zealand. Cochrane sent Gibson to Fiji in June 1938; his investigations led to work beginning on the construction of aerodromes at Nandi and Nausori.

The New Zealand Pacific Aviation Survey Expedition (NZPASE) was created in October, to be led by Gibson. The British Government, with a view to heading off the Americans, asked that Christmas, Nukunono and Hull Islands be added to the survey and for Christmas Island to be claimed for Britain. These were part of the plan for a commercial trans-Pacific TEAL (Tasman Empire Airways Limited) flying boat route from Auckland. To ensure the U.S. Government didn't get wind of the British moves, the expedition was classified 'Top Secret'; so secret that its leader Gibson, still working in Suva, wasn't told about it.

On 7 November, Cochrane sailed out of Auckland with the core of the team on HMS *Leander* on what had been publicly termed a 'Pacific Islands Cruise'. Others joined them in Suva, Fiji, and it was only then Gibson was told of his appointment. The full purpose of the expedition was not disclosed to the wider party until after they had sailed out of Suva on the 17th.[13]

Leander's tight schedule was a problem for Gibson so he had arranged for a second vessel, *Yanawai*, which allowed the group to continue its work into February 1939. They identified and surveyed several land aerodromes and flying boat landing areas across the key islands. Two airfields each were to be built in Fiji and Tonga with fuel and ammunition reserves for visiting aircraft.

Cochrane returned to Suva with *Leander* on 5 December and arrived back in Auckland on the 12th, the warship 'attacked' as it came into the Rangitoto Channel by RNZAF Blackburn Baffins based at Hobsonville.

The expedition was extremely useful and timely. The New Zealand-instigated Pacific Defence Conference held the following April in Wellington would reinforce the strategic importance of the islands, in particular Fiji, and allocate responsibility to New Zealand for air reconnaissance in the area from the New Hebrides to Fiji and Tonga. Gibson's interim NZPASE report proved invaluable.

Cochrane spent Christmas at home with the family in Wellington and then holidayed at Wanaka. His vital contribution to New Zealand's air defences was recognised by a grateful government with a CBE in the New Year's Honours.

On 16 February, the British Air Ministry dropped a bombshell: all overseas Torpedo Bomber and General Reconnaissance squadrons were to be equipped with the new Bristol Beaufort, which would not commence manufacture for another three months, with offshore production also to be set up in Australia. Despite the first Wellingtons being on the production line, Cochrane was asked to take Beauforts instead.

Despite strong opposition within the Ministry, over the next month Cochrane managed to re-state his case for the Wellington's suitability, in particular its superior armament, bomb load and, critically, range.

On 15 March, British Chief of Air Staff Sir Cyril Newall cabled Cochrane, finally agreeing to allow the Wellington purchase to go ahead.

Group Captain Hugh Saunders arrived in Auckland on 25 February to replace Cochrane, whose two-year term as Chief of the Air Staff had expired. Cochrane immediately flew him on a tour of the country in the PWD's Miles Whitney Straight, calling in at Ohakea on the 28th, Wigram on 2 March, and arriving in Wellington on the 4th.

Saunders took up the role of Chief of the Air Staff on the 9th and Cochrane and his family began to prepare for the trip home. After a final ten days of fishing near Rotorua and a round of farewells in Wellington, they sailed for England on the 25th, 'hoping that we should reach England before war broke out'.[14]

Events would soon show just how critical Cochrane's efforts were in setting up the organisation and expansion of the RNZAF, just in time for the greatest ever challenge to New Zealand's defences. In the meantime, Prime Minister Savage summarised the nation's gratitude:

> It casts no reflection on the work of others to suggest that in the future it will be said that military aviation in New Zealand 'began with Cochrane'.

~ ~ ~ ~ ~ ~ ~ ~

Notes & References

1. *Annual Report of the General Officer Commanding New Zealand Military Forces*, year ended 31st of May 1936, NZ Government, Appendices to the Journals of House of Representatives (and the Votes & Proceedings), PapersPast, National Library of New Zealand.

2. 'Splendid Record – Expert on Air Defence', *Auckland Star*, 13 October 1936.

3. Richard Mead, *Dambuster-in-Chief: The Life of Air Chief Marshal Sir Ralph Cochrane*, Pen & Sword Books Limited, 2020, p.42.

4. Air Chief Marshal Sir Ralph Cochrane's notes, written from memory during 1976, Air Force Museum of New Zealand, 86/111-3.

5. Diary of Wing Commander R.A. Cochrane, 20 November 1936 – 14 April 1937, Air Force Museum of New Zealand, 86/111-4.

6. T.M. Wilkes (Wing Commander), Report: Defence of New Zealand, 1936, AIR 1 102/3/3.

7. R.A. Cochrane, Report on the air aspect of the defence problems of New Zealand, including the suggested duties, strength and organization of the New Zealand Air Force, December 1936, 1. 102/4/1, Archives New Zealand.

8. Brian J. Hewson, 'Goliath's Apprentice – The Royal New Zealand Air Force and the United States in the Pacific Air War 1941–1945', published thesis, University of Canterbury, 2012.

9. W. David McIntyre, *New Zealand Prepares for War*, University of Canterbury Press, 1988.

10. 'New 'Planes', *Auckland Star*, 25 August 1937.

11. Grant Newman, 'Airships over Ohakea: What might have been', *The Aero Historian*, August 2022.

12. 'Defence Expansion', *New Zealand Herald*, 18 May 1938.

13. Felicity Caird, 'The Strategic Significance of the Pacific Islands in New Zealand's Defence Policy, 1935-1939', published thesis, University of Canterbury, 1987, p.103.

14. For a more detailed account of Cochrane's time in New Zealand see Brian Lockstone's book, *Into Wind ... The birth of the RNZAF*, Air Force Museum (N.Z.), 2007.

Bringing the Bombers Back

Ordering the Wellingtons from a manufacturer on the other side of the world was one thing; delivery was another.

The Airspeed Oxford trainers were able to be shipped from England in large wooden cases (with outer wings and tail removed), unloaded at Auckland port and barged up the harbour to Hobsonville for re-assembly. The Wellingtons, however, were too large and too complex in construction to be sent this way. Instead, plans were made to fly them from England to New Zealand, halfway round the world.

Regular commercial flights between England and Australia had started four years earlier, but nobody had ever attempted delivery flights of multiple aircraft over such a great distance – 13,000 miles. Five ferry flights were to be undertaken, each of six aircraft, from England to New Zealand via Singapore and Australia, refuelling at Royal Air Force (RAF) stations along the way.

The crews were to be made up of New Zealanders where possible, and the government made arrangements with the Air Ministry to release around 40 officers from the large numbers of New Zealanders already serving in England with the RAF, each with between two and five years of service experience.[1]

The Royal New Zealand Air Force (RNZAF) called on some of its most experienced pilots to lead the project. Squadron Leader Maurice 'Buck' Buckley MBE was sent to England in June 1937 on an exchange posting with the RAF, to gain experience on Wellingtons, head up a new ferry flight training unit in England and lead the first ferry flight out to New Zealand.

Born in 1895 in Seacliff, Otago, Maurice William Buckley attended Albury School and Timaru Boys High School. After leaving school, he worked on the family farm and made a name for himself racing motorbikes. In the First World War, he worked his way by sea to England and, in 1916, joined the Royal Naval Air Service (RNAS), training as a pilot. He served in the Eastern Mediterranean with No. 2 Wing, based initially at Mitylene on the Greek island of Lesbos. This involved long-distance scouting, reconnaissance, bombing, aerial photography and artillery observation over Turkey, and later Bulgaria, flying Maurice Farmans, Bristol Scouts and Sopwith Pups, Strutters and Camels.

On 20 July 1917, on the way back from bombing Smyrna, Buckley's Sopwith 1½ Strutter suffered engine failure and crashed into the sea near Mitylene. Briefly trapped underwater in the cockpit, he managed to escape and cling to the tail long enough to be rescued by a French trawler. On 30 November, Buckley was invalided out of Greece to Malta, and then England, with recurring malaria. While recuperating, he was granted medical leave to return (very briefly) to New Zealand.

Recovered and back in England again, he was passed fit and promoted to captain in the newly formed RAF, serving as a flight commander with No. 212 Squadron at Yarmouth for the last three months of the war. He remained in the RAF on the active reserve until May 1920.

After his return to New Zealand, Buckley became chief pilot for a new aviation venture – the New Zealand Aero Transport Company, Timaru – involved in joy riding flights and pioneering attempts to establish regular mail and passenger services. He was the first pilot to fly over Foveaux Strait, the most southerly flight ever attempted at the time, dropping mail and newspapers on Stewart Island.

'Buck' Buckley (left), mechanic Bill Harrington and deputy chairman Charles Howard Hewlett, alongside an Avro 504K owned by the Canterbury (NZ) Aviation Co Ltd, 1921. (Alexander Turnbull Library)

After reports of allegedly dangerous flying over Timaru, he and friend and fellow ex-RNAS pilot Philip 'Shorty' Fowler were charged with unauthorised 'trick-flying' (aerobatics) and low-level flying, new offences that had been added to the Aviation Act that year. Despite the 'nose-diving' described in court by a police sergeant, it turned out the two were simply investigating the beach as a potential landing place. The judge, however, found them guilty of low-altitude flying, a first for New Zealand, and fined them 20 shillings each.

In November 1921, Buckley moved to another joy riding operation, the Canterbury Aviation Company, based at Sockburn near Christchurch. He and his mechanic Bill Harrington made the first flights to Motueka and Westport (the latter ending embarrassingly in a swamp!) and, later, the first passenger-carrying flight from Gisborne to Auckland.

In 1923, Buckley formed his own business, The Arrow Aviation Company, operating joy rides during the West Coast Exhibition at Hokitika, up and down the West Coast and over the glaciers in his Avro 504K *Blazing Arrow*. It was at the end of this stint that he and Harrington made history by becoming the first to fly across the Southern Alps, making the 128-mile trip from Greymouth to Wigram (the new name for Sockburn) in one and three-quarter hours on 4 June 1924.

In June 1926, following two years back working on the family farm at Fairlie, and having attended the last three New Zealand Permanent Air Force (NZPAF) refresher courses, he joined the NZPAF, appointed as a flying instructor based at Wigram with the rank of captain.

As one of the senior pilots at Wigram, Buckley began to make a name for himself in the fledgling service. On 11 September 1928, he led an Air Force escort for Fokker F.VIIb/3m *Southern Cross* into Wigram at the triumphant conclusion of the first-ever flight across the Tasman Sea (by Charles Kingsford Smith, Charles Ulm and crew), then accompanied them on a publicity tour of the main centres of New Zealand. He joined the crew for test flights over Christchurch and for the flight up to Blenheim in preparation for their return flight to Sydney.

Later that year, the dashing Captain Buckley made the newspapers again when he and his new bride, Pat (a former 'Miss Manawatu' beauty queen and contestant in the first-ever 'Miss New Zealand' competition), wowed the crowds as they took off from Fielding, looped the loop and departed for the South Island on New Zealand's 'first aerial honeymoon'. On the way south, he handed the controls over to Pat and she became the first woman to fly across Cook Strait.

In 1929, Buckley took over as officer in command of Wigram aerodrome. Between 1926 and 1936, he was instrumental in the Air Force's pioneering work in aerial photography and photographic surveying and mapping. He was also heavily involved in aerial-relief efforts for the 1929 Murchison and 1931 Napier earthquakes. In June 1935, he was posted to Hobsonville, near Auckland, as Officer Commanding No. 1 Bomber Reconnaissance Flight (Vildebeest), promoted to flight lieutenant and awarded the MBE, the first such honour received by a member of the RNZAF.

It was during this period that he first met Wing Commander Ralph Cochrane, newly arrived from England and about to take up his new role as Chief of the Air Staff. On 4 January 1937, Buckley flew Cochrane in a Moth from Rotorua, where he had been on holiday, to Auckland.

Later that year, Buckley was promoted to squadron leader and put in command of Hobsonville station. Once again, he had a front-row seat in New Zealand aviation history when he drove the fast speedboat that cleared an Auckland harbour landing area for the arrival of Captain Edwin Musick's Pan American Airways *Samoan Clipper* flying boat from San Francisco on 30 March. Five days later, both Buckley and Cochrane were VIP passengers on the aircraft for a four-hour promotional flight south to Napier and return.

In June, Buckley was one of two RNZAF officers posted to England on exchange with the RAF. His duties included evaluation of suitable multi-engine trainers (which he carried out on arrival), familiarisation with the Vickers Wellington, and assistance with arrangements for purchase and delivery. He would then head up the project to bring back the aircraft for Cochrane's two new bomber squadrons. His duties included evaluation of the Vickers Wellington (and a suitable multi-engine trainer), as well as familiarisation and arrangements for purchase and delivery of the Wellingtons.

On 17 May 1938, he had his first flight in a Wellington, a 45-minute test flight with Vickers test pilot 'Mutt' Summers at Martlesham Heath. This was the first Wellington Mark I, L4212, a pre-production machine, only the second built and still undergoing testing and trials.

In the meantime, Buckley's exchange role had him serving firstly with No. 166 Squadron, and then with No. 97 Squadron on Handley Page Heyford bombers, followed by a navigation course at Hamble. On 18 November, he was posted to No. 38 Squadron, based at RAF Marham, the second RAF squadron to operate the new Wellingtons. There, Buckley served as a flight commander and, briefly, between wing commanders, as acting commanding officer.

By early 1939, he was ready for his next role, leading the largest and longest ferry flight ever attempted.

The first Vickers Wellington Mark I, L4212, Heathrow, 8 May 1938. (Joe Connolly/Air-Britain Photographic Images Collection)

~ ~ ~ ~ ~ ~ ~ ~

Back in New Zealand, Flight Lieutenant Cyril Kay had been selected as Buckley's second in command, with the role of ferry training navigation officer.

Cyril Eyton Kay was born in 1902 and grew up in Devonport, Auckland, where he enjoyed sailing. A flight with one of the early barnstormers, while still at secondary school, inspired him to become a pilot. He applied to join the RNZAF, but at that time only refresher training for existing pilots was available, so he worked his passage to Britain and tried to enlist in the RAF. In search of a referee, he approached the former New Zealand governor-general, Lord Jellicoe, against whom he had once won a sailing race. Jellicoe wrote, 'if Cyril Kay is as good in the air as he is on the sea, he will be an acquisition to the Royal Air Force'. Kay entered the RAF on a five-year short-service commission on 14 July 1926.

Kay specialised in navigation and meteorology and, in 1928, was elected a Fellow of the Royal Meteorological Society. In 1929, he flew in the RAF Air Pageant set-piece displays at Hendon.

In 1930, while still serving with the RAF, he and fellow New Zealander Flying Officer Harold 'Pip' Piper flew a tiny Desoutter monoplane from Croydon, England, to Darwin in an unsuccessful attempt to break the England–Australia record. The following year, he attended the Wasserkuppe gliding school, the 'birthplace of gliding' in Germany, and achieved the rare distinction for 'an Englishman' of securing a 'C' gliding certificate in Germany. He then became an instructor at a flying school in Digby, Lincolnshire.

Kay returned to New Zealand in 1932, working in commercial aviation, and was involved in the establishment of Kay Robot Air-Pilots Ltd to commercialise the compact compressed-air autopilot device he had invented. The technology was unfortunately overtaken by the gyroscopic stabiliser about 18 months later.

In 1934, he competed in the MacRobertson centenary air race from England to Australia, with Squadron Leader Jim Hewett and wireless operator/photographer Frank Stewart. Their entry was New Zealand-backed and they flew a twin-engine de Havilland Dragon Rapide (*Tainui*, ZK-ACO, Race No. 60), into fifth place. They then flew on from Sydney to Palmerston North, completing the first flight from England to New Zealand and becoming the first New Zealand crew to cross the Tasman Sea by air.

Cyril Kay and Harold Piper, at the time of their England–Australia record attempt, 1930. (National Library of Australia)

Kay joined the RNZAF as a flying officer in July 1935 and became chief navigation instructor at No. 1 Flying Training School, Wigram. Usually known as 'Cyrus', Kay was described as a superb instructor and a brilliant and daring pilot. His combination of navigational skills and experience of long-distance flights made him an ideal candidate to help Buckley organise and lead the Wellington ferry flights.

~ ~ ~ ~ ~ ~ ~ ~

In April 1939, volunteers for the ferry flights had been called for from the several hundred New Zealand officers already serving in England on short-service commissions in the RAF and from any at the end of their term, now on the reserve. Any New Zealander in the RAF under the age of 28 and holding the rank of airman pilot was eligible and, if selected, they would be commissioned as pilot officers in the RNZAF before leaving Britain. In return, they were required to stay on for a fixed term of five years, an effective way for the RNZAF to repatriate some of New Zealand's best and brightest. At the same time, RNZAF airmen and technicians were sent to England for specialised training in maintenance and servicing of the new Wellington bombers.

The plan was for the first group of officers and airmen to assemble in England in June and July of 1939 for three months' training in preparation for the first delivery flight to New Zealand. They would be based at RAF Marham, where Buckley had been serving with 38 Squadron. He would report to, and be assisted by, Squadron Leader Sid Wallingford, New Zealand Liaison Officer (NZLO) to the Air Ministry, who had been nominated to lead the third flight.

Sidney Wallingford was another hugely experienced New Zealand aviation pioneer, his career almost reading like a *Boys' Own* adventure. Born in 1898 in England, his family moved to New Zealand when he was 13; he attended Auckland Grammar School. His father had been an Olympic shooter and was the British Army's top marksman before transferring to the New Zealand Army in 1911 and earning a Military Cross at Gallipoli.

Just out of school, Sid had worked his way to England in 1916 and joined the Army, serving in the Balkans, before joining the Royal Flying Corps in 1918 and learning to fly in Egypt. After the war, he spent two years in the Fijian Police, then took up a short-service commission in the RAF, flying seaplanes and, following in his famous father's footsteps, becoming the RAF's rifle-shooting champion.

He returned to New Zealand in 1929 to serve with the NZPAF, posted to Hobsonville, the new seaplane base near Auckland. Wallingford had the distinction of flying the New Zealand Air Force's first-ever active operational sortie – a two-hour-and-50-minute reconnaissance in a Gipsy Moth seaplane around the island of Upolu, Western Samoa, trying to spot Mau rebels in the bush. Then, on 27 January 1930, he hand-delivered the Air Force's first bomb dropped in anger; a home-made gun-cotton device packed in a treacle tin. His target was a large boat thought to be carrying Mau members to Savaii but, fortunately, the 'bomb' failed to explode (the boat actually belonged to an Australian missionary!). In 1931, he was involved in the NZPAF's efforts to fly in medical and other supplies to Napier after the devastating earthquake.

Wallingford was critical of the country's air defences and submitted a report in 1933, 'Treatise on the Question of an Air Force for New Zealand' in which he stated the Permanent Air Force was 'useless as an active force and would be a hindrance if sent overseas in its present state', arguing it gave the public a false sense of security and that new suitable aircraft were needed.[2]

Then, in 1935, he captured the public's imagination when he landed a Fairey IIIF seaplane beyond the breakers at Karekare Beach on Auckland's West Coast to rescue a woman, Hazel Bentham, who had been swept out sea beyond the reach of the surf-rescue teams which had made several unsuccessful attempts to reach her during the four hours she was in the water.

Wallingford attended the RAF Staff College at Andover in 1936 and then took up the position of NZLO, based in London. The role included military procurement on behalf of the New Zealand Government, so Wallingford was closely involved in the Wellington project.

Now he would be helping Buckley with planning as well as training for the ferry flights back home.

~ ~ ~ ~ ~ ~ ~ ~

The success or failure of the Wellington delivery project sat largely on the shoulders of Maurice Buckley. He carried the responsibility for organising, training and leading the pioneering first ferry flight, and for planning and setting up a system to assemble and train the subsequent ferry flights. He would also carry out much of the Wellington conversion of the first batch of pilots.

'Buck' was a quiet, determined character with a low-key, empathetic leadership style others would later describe as 'fatherly'. He didn't seek the limelight and led by example. It was Buck's vision, drive and ability to improvise with the limited resources available that shaped the unit, and it was his down-to-earth approach and cheerful positivity that generated spirit, camaraderie and, in time, a fierce loyalty in his men.

Flight Lieutenant Sid Wallingford (right) and his commanding officer, Squadron Leader Len Isitt, were both involved in the dramatic rescue at Karekare on 3 February 1935. (Wallingford collection)

By the first week in May 1939, his fledgling organisation was starting to take shape at Marham. The unit was allocated two hangars, Hangars 67 and 69, together with three rooms and an armoury in Hangar 67, and one barrack room. Room 17, Hangar 67, was to be the flight commander's office, and a telephone was installed.[3]

As he later wrote, referring to himself in the third person:[4]

> On the 4th of May a storekeeper arrived, and a Flight Sergeant from No. 9 Squadron, and during May other N.C.O's [*sic*] and airmen came along to complete the staff. Not a lot could be done at this stage, as the S/Ldr had his Flight duties to attend to as well as preparing for the coming job.
>
> Our headquarters were two offices and a store, empty. No aeroplanes, no tables, no chairs, no stationery and no place to 'demand' them.

He was particularly keen to get hold of his aeroplanes.

~ ~ ~ ~ ~ ~ ~ ~

Notes & References

1. Report by the Chief of Air Staff for the Year Ended 31st of March 1939, NZ Government, Appendices to the Journals of House of Representatives (and the Votes & Proceedings), PapersPast, National Library of New Zealand.

2. Brian J. Hewson, 'Goliath's Apprentice – The Royal New Zealand Air Force and the United States in the Pacific Air War 1941–1945', published thesis, 2012, p.129.

3. Formation of New Zealand Air Force Squadron at Royal Air Force Station, Marham, letter from Station Commander RAF Marham, 24 April 1939, M.W. Buckley collection.

4. Personal narrative, formation of the New Zealand Squadron, M.W. Buckley collection.

The Wellingtons

The new Wellington bombers were being built by Vickers-Armstrongs Limited at their Weybridge factory on the outskirts of London, also site of the famous Brooklands motor racing track.

The Royal New Zealand Air Force's (RNZAF) first 18 machines were ordered under Contract No. 781439/38, dated 19 November 1938, to come out of the very first order placed by the Royal Air Force (RAF) for 180 Mark I models (Contract No. 549268/36). Air Liaison Officer Sidney Wallingford had negotiated the allocation of three production blocks of six aircraft each, blocks chosen to coincide with the timing of ferry flight crew training. The first block would be the 100th–105th Wellingtons produced against this order, anticipating delivery in April 1939.

The first Mark I carried the serial number L4212, so the first New Zealand Wellington was L4311. A photograph survives of L4311 sitting on the production line, nearing completion, already wearing its RNZAF serial number NZ300.

Another wonderfully detailed photo survives of its cockpit, with dual controls and the manufacturer's data plate clearly visible. These images are probably from a set issued for publicity purposes by Vickers-Armstrongs around May–June 1939, as details of the new bomber had, until then, been on 'the secret list'. Some appeared in detailed feature articles introducing the Wellington, published at the time by both *The Aeroplane* and *Flight* magazines.

NZ300 (nearest), the first of the RNZAF's new Wellingtons, on the production line at the Vickers Weybridge factory, March–April 1939. (via Geoff Oliver)

The cockpit of Vickers Wellington Mark I NZ300 (dual control), the first built for the RNZAF by Vickers-Armstrong. (*The Aeroplane*)

NZ300's data plate behind the right-hand control column reads 'Type 403, No. NZ300. Built at Weybridge Works. Date April 1939 England'. (*The Aeroplane*)

The aircraft's design benefitted from Vickers-Armstrongs' experience in long-distance flights. Chief designer Rex Pierson had designed the Vickers Vimy bomber which made the first non-stop crossing of the Atlantic in June 1919, flown by John Alcock (who Maurice Buckley had served with in Greece in 1917) and Arthur Whitten Brown. Later that year, another Vimy made the first flight from England to Australia, flown by brothers Ross and Keith Smith and mechanics James Bennett and Wally Shiers. Then, in 1938, three Vickers Wellesley monoplane bombers of the RAF's Long Range Development Unit had broken the non-stop flight record, making the 7,158-mile trip from Egypt to Australia in one hop. The Wellesley was the predecessor to the Wellington, designed by Pierson, and the first RAF aircraft to employ Barnes Wallis's geodetic construction principle.[1]

Buckley and the RNZAF had developed a close relationship with Vickers and the first six RNZAF Wellingtons were manufactured to the RNZAF's own specification, designated Type 403. The RNZAF's 'special features' were treated by Vickers as 'extras' on top of the standard RAF specification and fit out. They included long-distance fuel tanks and a fuel system with jettison capability, long-distance oil tanks, an air (flotation) system, outer flares, and extra fuselage fairings. The flotation system involved 14 canvas bags located in the bomb bay, to be inflated by carbon-dioxide cylinders after the bombs and fuel had been jettisoned and the bomb bay doors closed. The 'extras' added a cost of £1,112.00 to the base price of £15,250.00 for each aircraft.[2]

In its 6 July 1939 issue, *Flight* magazine reported:

> The Wellingtons for New Zealand are having flotation bags installed in their bomb compartments for the delivery flight, and arrangements are made in these machines to jettison the fuel from the wing tanks which, when empty, supply a very useful measure of flotation.

The first six aircraft were intended for the training of ferry crews and five of them were fitted with dual controls for pilot instruction. They were supplied with all unnecessary equipment removed as they were primarily intended for training and, only later, for ferrying. Buckley described them as 'skeletons'.

Wireless was not fitted and, although they had Vickers gun turrets (front and rear), no guns were supplied.[3] These aircraft were to stay on in England for the meantime, while the second batch of six delivered would make the first ferry flight out to New Zealand.

Originally, the second batch (NZ306–11) were to be Wellington Mark Is, numbers 148 to 153 off the production line. However, a change had been made to the order sometime around January 1939, upgrading the second and third batches to Mark IA models, also with the RNZAF specification 'extras', designated Type 412.

Because the Mark I could not be easily modified to IA specification[4], the next six had to be moved to a block of Mark IAs under the same RAF contract (No. 549268/36). These machines were to be produced from consecutive Air Ministry serial numbers N2874 to N2879. One of this second batch of 'NZ' Wellingtons was to be fitted with a revolutionary top-secret piece of equipment.

Dr Ernest Marsden, Director of New Zealand's Department of Scientific & Industrial Research, had arrived in England in April at the invitation of the British Government to learn about new radio direction finding (RDF) technology. The development of RDF (what would later come to be known as radar) was highly secret, but the British were keen to share their findings with some of the 'Dominions' before war broke out in case their research facilities and personnel were lost to Germany.

Marsden was given the job of evaluating the different types of radar under development to choose the most appropriate for New Zealand's wartime needs and bring back whatever information and equipment he could. With the new knowledge, the plan was for New Zealand to, as quickly as possible, develop and manufacture its own radar.[5]

As war grew ever more likely, Marsden had to weigh up his wish to bring back the most up-to-date developments (in a rapidly evolving science) against the urgent need to get home and start work. In May, he wrote back to the government suggesting New Zealand should start identifying and training specialists to work on this new programme and appoint a committee to direct development.

Of the types being worked on in Britain, Air-to-Surface Vessel (ASV) radar was of particular interest and directly relevant to the main threat New Zealand faced – attack by sea. It was already in limited use with the RAF. Based at New Zealand House, Marsden worked closely with Liaison Officer Wallingford so was aware the Wellingtons were due to fly back to New Zealand and that, in their intended maritime role, they would eventually be equipped with some form of ASV. On 6 June, he recommended ASV units be installed in two of the first flight Wellingtons and that he fly back to New Zealand in one of them to observe the effectiveness of the new technology on the way.

Meanwhile, the first of the new Wellingtons was rolling off the Weybridge assembly line.

Before delivery, each aircraft had to be test flown at Weybridge by Vickers-Armstrongs' test pilots, Flight Lieutenants Joseph 'Mutt' Summers and Maurice Hare, so it seems likely NZ300 was first flown in mid-April. On 25 April, it was flown from Weybridge to an unknown airfield for a ceremonial handover of the first Wellington to New Zealand Government representatives to be held on the 27th.[6] After the handover, NZ300 was flown back to Weybridge. The round trip used 330 gallons of fuel and 28 gallons of oil, separately itemised and charged by Vickers.

According to the original plan, the first aircraft would be delivered on 29 April, and five more by the end of May. In fact, optimistic newspaper reports back in New Zealand were predicting the first ferry flight would leave England in early June! However, no more aircraft were delivered over the next four weeks and NZ300 remained at Weybridge.

'New Zealand's Modern Bombers Undergo Trials.' An RNZAF Wellington takes off on a test flight at Weybridge, May 1939. The Wellington Mark II in the foreground is a later model, at that time still under development. (*Otago Daily Times*, 12 June 1939)

Mutt Summers took it up for a 20-minute test flight at 4:20 in the afternoon on 19 May, with Robert 'Bob' Handasyde on board as flight test observer. Although there is no record of a technical issue, the aircraft was held back for a series of further test flights in July and August. At least three of these were fuel-jettison tests.

The fuel-jettison system introduced compressed air into the four main sets of wing tanks, forcing the fuel out through jettison valves and outlet pipes extending aft under the wing and exiting near (but projecting beyond) the outboard end of the flaps. A full tank could be jettisoned in nine minutes with the flaps up, or six minutes with the flaps down. By closing the jettison valve afterwards, the empty, air-filled tanks provided buoyancy in a ditching.

One fuel-jettison test was carried out on 25 July with Hare as pilot and Summers flying alongside in another Wellington, L4388, so photographs could be taken. Two more jettison tests were flown on 24 and 25 August with test flight observer Bob Rampling on board. Paraffin was used instead of petrol and different jettison pipes and flap settings were tried.[7]

The fact that Vickers was, at the same time, producing Mark IA machines with a functioning fuel-jettison system as standard suggests there were difficulties getting a system that would work properly with early production Mark Is. This could be why the remaining serial numbers from that original first production block – L4312 to L4316 – were cancelled and never built. Instead, NZ301 to NZ305 were re-allocated to individual non-consecutive airframes from the next block of 75 Mark I RAF serial numbers (L4317 to L4391). As it turned out, the second 'NZ' Wellington to be manufactured was L4330, delivered as NZ301.

NZ300 remained at Weybridge. Frustratingly for Buckley, it meant another month before he could get his hands on a Wellington.

Finally, the big day arrived – Wednesday 24 May 1939. At 4:20pm, Buckley and Wallingford, with Pilot Officer Arthur Rose-Price as navigator, took off from Weybridge in Wellington NZ301 to make the 50-minute delivery flight to Marham. Rose-Price was a young English pilot who Buckley had flown with at No. 38 Squadron, and was the brother of Dennis Price, the movie actor. Appreciating the significance of the moment, Buckley noted in his logbook 'Collecting 1st NZ Wellington from Weybridge'.

The same afternoon, pilot Flying Officer John Hopkins and navigator Pilot Officer Ian Cross (both from 38 Squadron) flew a second Wellington, NZ302 (L4340), across from Vickers Weybridge, landing at 5:00pm. It must have been an exciting moment for Buckley and his small team – two brand-new aircraft parked on the airfield, the impressive first components of the RNZAF's new bomber squadrons.

The following day, Group Captain Ralph Cochrane visited Marham. He had arrived back in England in April and was dropping in on Buckley to see how the ferry flight project was shaping up. Buckley took him up for a 25-minute spin in NZ302.

Cochrane too would have felt a great sense of satisfaction, to see his bold plan starting to take shape. Two days later, he reported to the Air Ministry in London to take up his new posting as Deputy Director of Intelligence.

However, by the end of May, Buckley still had only the two Wellingtons.

The first pilots and technicians arrived in early June, and training commenced with the first dual instruction on the 6th. Three more Wellingtons eventually arrived later that month: NZ303 (L4350) on the 14th, NZ304 (L4355) on the 20th and NZ305 (L4360) on the 29th.

NZ300 never made it to Marham. For now, Buckley had to make do with just five Wellingtons.

~ ~ ~ ~ ~ ~ ~ ~

RNZAF Wellingtons near completion at the Vickers-Armstrongs Weybridge factory, April or May 1939. NZ302 is second closest to the camera, fitted with an astrodome. The banked Brooklands racetrack can be seen in the background. (*Flight*, 6 July 1939)

Notes & References

1. Derek O'Connor, 'Flight of the Wellesleys', *HistoryNet*, at https://www.historynet.com/flight-of-the-wellesleys/.

2. H.L. Wonfor, Letter, Vickers-Armstrongs to Air Ministry, 16 May 1940, GBR/0012/MS Vickers Doc 403, Cambridge University Library.

3. Interestingly, for such a small batch of aircraft built to the same specification and with relatively close (RAF) serial numbers, photographs show some variation. At least two (NZ300 and NZ302) had a hard, straight demarcation line between the standard RAF camouflage scheme and the black underside, while NZ303 and NZ304 had a hard, wavy demarcation line, and one appears to have had a "mirror" camo' scheme. At least one (NZ302) had a Perspex astrodome fitted, whereas the others appear to have had the Mark I's more usual sliding hatch in that position. The standard RAF roundel with wide yellow outer ring was applied to the fuselage and large white 'NZ' serial numbers were marked under the wings.

4. Structural changes in the Mark IA design included a slightly larger, strengthened airframe, new front and rear gun turrets, allowance for a ventral turret, a new "power egg" engine nacelle to accommodate modular engine upgrades, a larger wheel and stronger undercarriage.

5. DSIR [Department of Scientific and Industrial Research] World War 2 Narratives. No 3. Radar. Copy No. 3, Archives New Zealand.

6. 'First Flight to Leave in October', *The Press*, 27 April 1939.

7. Vickers-Armstrongs Ltd Flight Reports, Brooklands Museum, via Andy Wilson.

The New Zealand Squadron

On 1 June 1939, the ferry flight training unit was officially established under Buckley's command for the purpose of assembling and working up the delivery flights, as announced in the *New Zealand Gazette*:[1]

> A temporary unit in the United Kingdom is formed, to be called the New Zealand Squadron, with headquarters at the Royal Air Force Station, Marham, King's Lynn, Norfolk.

The structure of the new squadron had been laid out in a letter from Group Captain APV Daly, Station Commander RAF Marham, to the Officer Commanding, No. 38 (B) Squadron on 24 April.[2] It was to be divided into two flights; a 'Permanent Flight', made up of administrative and maintenance personnel, and a 'Mobile Flight', i.e., the ferry flight personnel:

> The Officer Commanding the Squadron is responsible for the organisation, training and despatch of Flights. His responsibility for the Permanent Flight is to cease on his departure from the United Kingdom with the Mobile Flight and is to be taken over by the officer detailed to command the following Mobile Flight who will then become the succeeding Officer Commanding, New Zealand Squadron.
>
> The Officer Commanding the Squadron will come directly under the New Zealand Liaison Officer, Air Ministry regarding all matters of training, organisation and despatch.

While the unit would 'come under Headquarters, Bomber Command for administration, discipline, accounting and pay', Buckley would effectively report directly to Wallingford.

The squadron was only intended to have a life of about 18 months, co-located at Marham with two operational Wellington units, Nos. 38 and 115 Squadrons. The Permanent Flight would have 33 personnel, mostly Royal Air Force (RAF) technical staff with experience on Wellingtons, to be paid at RAF rates. An 'advance party' of eight had been formed as a nucleus for the new unit on 21 April. Two of these were New Zealand fitters; Corporals Thomas Read and William 'Bill' Steven, already at Marham working on Wellingtons, having transferred to 38 Squadron from the New Zealand-crewed Royal Navy cruiser HMS *Achilles*, where they had serviced Supermarine Walrus amphibious aircraft.

The Permanent Flight had to manage a rolling intake and output of aeroplanes, pilots, aircrews and associated wireless and engineering specialists as each mobile flight of six aircraft and crews was received, equipped, trained up and then ferried to New Zealand at two-monthly intervals. Stores and equipment would be loaned or hired from maintenance units and the parent station, RAF Marham.

The mobile flights would be made up of Royal New Zealand Air Force (RNZAF) pilots and mixed RAF–RNZAF crews, all on RNZAF rates of pay. The 1st Mobile Flight nominated 12 RNZAF pilots and six RNZAF technicians, so would require six RAF personnel; the 2nd Mobile Flight would need ten. The RAF men in each mobile flight had been recruited for up to two years and were to stay on in New Zealand to assist with maintenance of the Wellingtons and training of their RNZAF equivalents. However, on the day of its establishment, 1 June, the new squadron consisted of Buckley, one flight sergeant, one sergeant, six corporals, 12 mechanics and two aeroplanes.

Flight Sergeant Edwin Roberts, the senior RAF fitter, became Buckley's administration and procurement specialist. He taught himself to type on Buckley's personal typewriter and set out to obtain everything that was needed, initially using his contacts at No. 9 Squadron, his previous posting.

In early June, Buckley was joined by his second-in-command and navigating officer 'Cyrus' Kay, newly promoted to the rank of squadron leader. Kay had left Auckland for Sydney by sea on 16 May, and then

S/L Cyril 'Cyrus' Kay (left) and S/L Maurice 'Buck' Buckley MBE at Marham in August 1939.
(TO Freeman collection, Air Force Museum of NZ)

flew by Imperial Airways, arriving at Southampton on 30 May. His wife and family were on their way as well, completing the trip from Sydney by sea.

Three New Zealand pilots who had been on short-service commissions with the RAF also arrived: Acting Flight Lieutenant Aubrey 'Breck' Breckon, Flight Lieutenant Charles Hunter (who Buckley had instructed back in his Wigram days) and Flying Officer Arthur Greenaway. Buckley himself checked out each pilot on Wellingtons as they arrived – his logbook has him clocking up 24 instructional flights as captain in June. Breckon soon joined him as an instructor, registering four hours as captain that month among 12.10 hours in total. Pilots were tested to 'Solo', '1st Pilot Day Only (Wellington)' and 'Qualified to Carry Crew (Wellington)' standards. From August, '1st Pilot Night (Wellington)' tests were carried out.

Buckley flew across to Weybridge again on 14 June to collect the third new Wellington, NZ303, with F/O Greenaway as 2nd pilot and Wallingford as navigator. That was the end of Sid Wallingford's involvement in training. He had only managed a few flights as it appears he had to return to his duties as NZ Liaison Officer in London in mid-June due to the worsening situation in Europe - he would take no further part in flying.

Buckley collected the fourth Wellington, NZ304, on 20 June (with Breckon as 2nd pilot and Corporal Steven along for the ride), and NZ305 on the 29th (again with Breckon).

Meanwhile, Dr Ernest Marsden, Director of New Zealand's Department of Scientific & Industrial Research, had been busy building an Air-to-Surface Vessel (ASV) radar set at the Bawdsey Research Station, the main centre for RAF work on radio direction finding (RDF). On 30 June, he recommended ordering one set for installation in one of the Wellingtons, along with spares not available in New Zealand, at a cost of approximately £300. The early sets were quite large and virtually custom-built, more easily installed into an aircraft during construction than by retrofitting. Acting Prime Minister Walter Nash approved the order and took Marsden's recommendations to cabinet.

Seven more pilots arrived at Marham in July, all New Zealanders serving with the RAF: Flying Officers John Collins and John 'Jack' Adams, and Pilot Officers William 'Bill' Coleman, Trevor Freeman, Fred 'Popeye' Lucas, Neville Williams and Wilfred 'Bill' Williams.

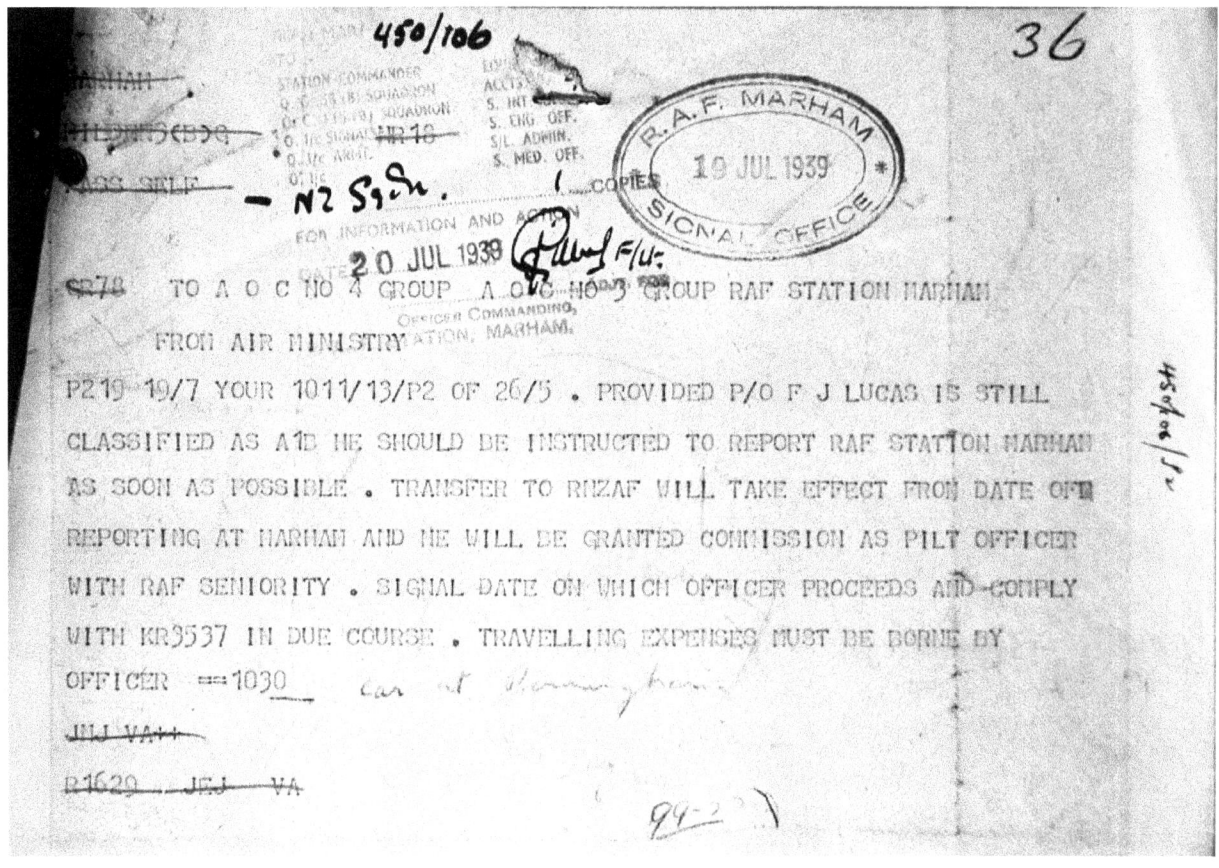

Telegram instruction from the Air Ministry advising the posting of Pilot Officer Fred 'Popeye' Lucas to the New Zealand Squadron at RAF Marham, and transfer from the RAF to the RNZAF, 19 July 1939. (Archives New Zealand)

Buckley continued to lead by example, clocking up another 53.45 hours as captain in July, all instructional flights, bar one petrol-consumption test. Breckon accumulated 43.40 hours as captain, with Greenaway (10.20 hours) and Collins (9.05 hours) also moving into the training captain's seat.

Back on 17 January, six RNZAF wireless specialists had departed Wellington on the passenger liner MS *Rangitane*, sent to England to train with various Wellington squadrons in the RAF before joining the ferry flights. They had arrived in London on 21 February. Five of them were from the very first class to graduate from the RNZAF's new Wireless School at Wigram. Two others from that class would follow six months later.

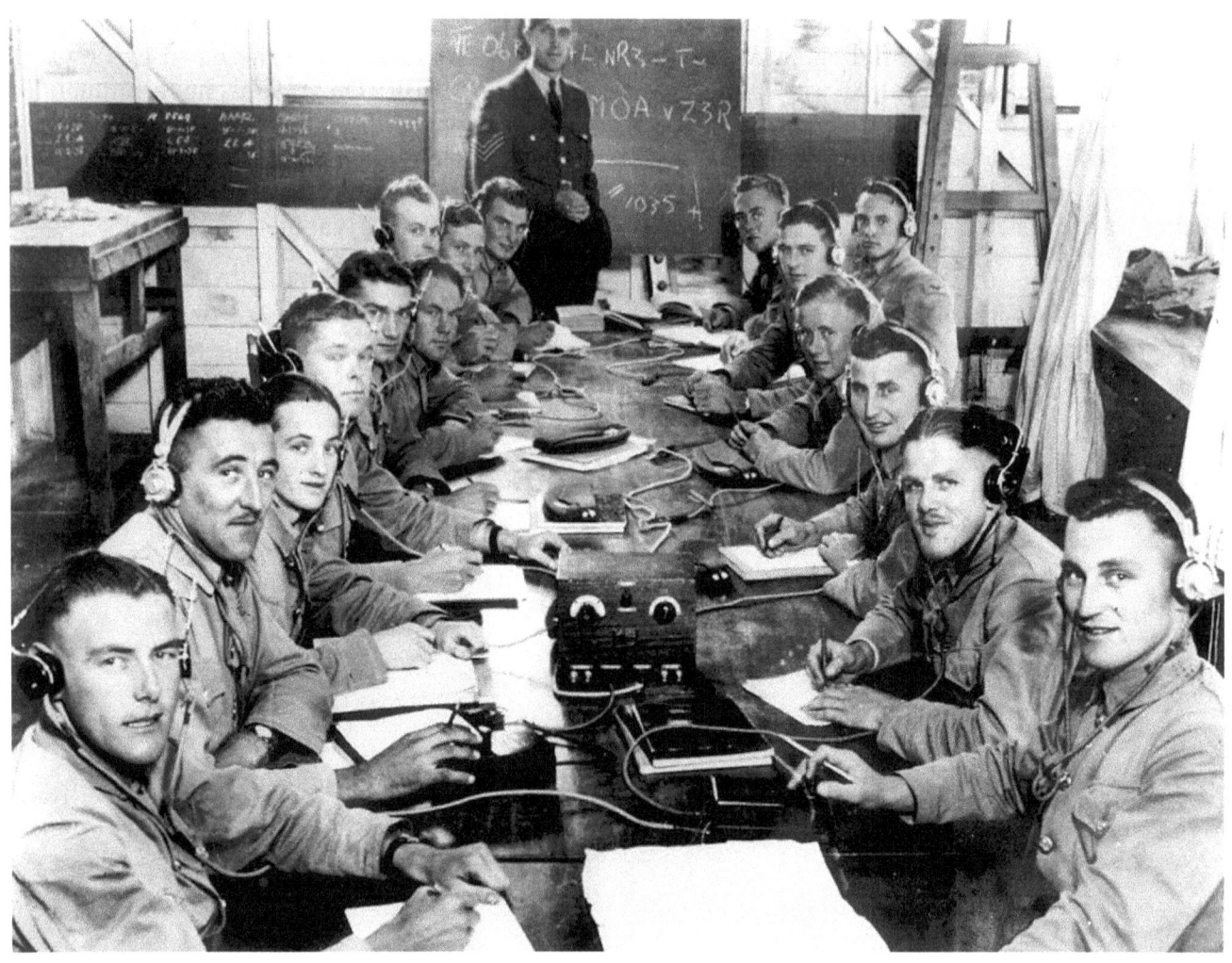

The first wireless course undergoing training at RNZAF Station Wigram, 1938
Left row, front to back: R Anderson, CBG Knight, AE Berry, DC McGlashan, BG Willis, FMB George, GO Perrott, DK Scriven, R Mitchell, Sergeant R Gibbs (instructor, standing).
Right row, front to back: DJ Cummings, JH Langridge, JT White, LD Davies, WVA Phear, AB Stichbury, RAJ Anderson.
(MUS961789, Air Force Museum of NZ)

Four from this group arrived to join the squadron in July: Aircraftmen First Class Ronald Anderson, Donald McGlashan and Joe White, and Leading Aircraftman Ted Williams. They had trained at Mildenhall with No. 99 Squadron RAF, which also operated Wellington Mark Is, and had been nominated to join the crews for the first ferry flight.

Aubrey Breckon received a promotion to flight lieutenant on 1 August. Breckon was the unit's photographic specialist, having followed in his father's footsteps as a photographer for the *New Zealand Herald* and the *Auckland Weekly News* before the war, with plenty of experience in aerial photography. On 11 August, he and Bill Coleman took Sergeant Evans, of the station photographic unit, and Sergeants Warren and Buck, up for a photographic survey of the aerodrome.

'Six wireless operators of the Royal New Zealand Air Force, who are proceeding to the United Kingdom to join the Vickers Wellington bombers which are to be flown from England to New Zealand.'
Top row, from left, Messrs. C. B. G. Knight, R. A. J. Anderson, J. H. Langridge. Bottom row, Messrs. D. C. McGlashan, E. P. Williams, and J.T. White. (*Evening Post*, 11 January 1939)

Flying training was now in full swing: dual instruction, local and cross-country flights, pilot testing, consumption and overload tank testing, blind flying, single-engine and forced landing practices. Pilot Officer Meyer-Williams RAF appeared regularly as a pilot on training flights, and a Sergeant Sach RAF was listed as a flying instructor and appears in crew lists at this time. These two were probably on loan from 38 Squadron as they were not included in the subsequent squadron move to Harwell.

Wellington NZ303, Marham, 10 July 1939. (RNZAF official via Andy Thomas)

Meanwhile, Marsden's Australian radar counterpart, Dr David Martyn, had stopped off in Wellington, New Zealand, on his way back from England en route to Sydney. At a top-secret meeting[3] with New Zealand Government and scientific representatives on 28 July, his positive impressions of the potential of RDF reinforced what Marsden had been saying. Regarding ASV, he stressed the fact that sets needed to be designed specifically for the aircraft type in which they are to be used and are not easily interchangeable between aircraft. He suggested a prompt order might get one prototype set by the end of the year.

On 2 August, Acting Prime Minister Walter Nash cabled London authorising up to four aircraft from the first flight be fitted with ASV and confirming Marsden should fly back with the first flight of Wellingtons.[4] He advised that Cabinet had approved expenditure of £29,000 sterling for new RDF technology, including 34 ASV sets, enough to equip the whole Wellington fleet.

Marsden replied on the 4th saying that, at that time, there were only six ASV sets in use in Britain and, with the intense pressure to supply the RAF, he was only able to secure one for installation in an RNZAF Wellington. As originally planned, he undertook to obtain critical components in Britain and bring them back to build a prototype ASV as the basis for the manufacture of sets in New Zealand.

Marsden had given Dr Martyn the New Zealand Government's copies of his confidential RDF reports to deliver when the Australian got to Wellington. Trans-Tasman co-operation in radar development got off to a bad start when Dr Martyn left for Sydney by sea, taking Marsden's reports with him!

~ ~ ~ ~ ~ ~ ~ ~

Notes & References

1. 'Formation and Designation of a Temporary Unit', Air Department, Wellington, 28 July 1939, *The New Zealand Gazette*, Numb. 59, August 3 1939.

2. Formation of New Zealand Air Force Squadron at Royal Air Force Station, Marham, letter from Station Commander RAF Marham, 24 April 1939, M.W. Buckley collection.

3. Defence of NZ – General – Report on meeting held in Mr Berendsen's Room (Address by Dr Martyn) – 28/7/39, Archway Item ID:R18871379, Archives New Zealand.

4. DSIR [Department of Scientific and Industrial Research] World War 2 Narratives. No 3. Radar. Copy No. 3, Reference: AAOQ 28051 W3424 16/, Archives New Zealand.

Preparations Back Home

The caption for this photograph of a Wellington in the *New Zealand Herald* of 27th July 1939 read:
'Personnel Announced For Flight of Wellington Bombers From England to New Zealand.
A Vickers Wellington twin-engined bomber in flight. Officers and airmen who are to bring the first formation of six of these machines to the Dominion have begun their training. The flight, first of a series of five, is expected to take off before October 1. Inset are portraits of Squadron-Leader [sic] W.M. Buckley (left) and Squadron-Leader S. Wallingford, commanding officers for two of the flights.'

In New Zealand, public interest in the ferry flights was strong and the press covered every development.

The 1st Mobile Flight was expected to leave the UK on 1 October 1939 and arrive in New Zealand on the 26th, landing at its new home, the brand-new station under construction at Ohakea; it would form the basis of No. 1 Squadron RNZAF.

In a letter to his mother back home, Pilot Officer Bill Coleman wrote:

> I hope to be back in New Zealand by the end of October ... I have transferred from the Royal Air Force, and now belong to the Royal New Zealand Air Force. I shall be a pilot and navigator on one of the first six machines, and we expect to take off from Marham here on October 1, and taking our time and nursing the engines, should be in New Zealand about October 26. We will be making for the new aerodrome at Ohakea, near Palmerston North, and are scheduled to arrive there from Sydney about that date.

The RNZAF's existing airfields and hangars were too small for the new bombers and mile-long runways were needed for the faster, heavier machines. Work started at Ohakea at the end of February 1938, constructing two huge new hangars and an airfield, with three shifts working round the clock.

Due to the shortage of structural steel in the country and the urgency of the project, new technologies were pioneered in hangar design and construction.[1] The hangars were designed by Charles Turner, chief designing engineer of the Public Works Department, and built by McMillan Bros Limited. At the time, they were by far the largest structures of this type built in New Zealand and said to be the largest hangars in the Southern Hemisphere. Each would be large enough to hold nine Wellingtons. The hangars were front opening with ten 25-foot high × 23-foot wide reinforced concrete sliding panel doors cast in place. Annexes for workshops, storerooms and offices were incorporated in the sides and rear of each building.

To enclose the 220 × 190-foot area of clear hangar space, ten huge roof-span arches of stressed concrete were created in place, with footings 300 feet apart. The arches, and the reinforced concrete roof sections between the arches, were poured progressively on top of a 240-ton forming structure that could be moved on rails. Concrete was hoisted from ground-level up to a massive overhead scaffolding structure and wheel-barrowed across to each pour, which was made symmetrically from both sides of the span, meeting in the middle. A pour could take between 24 and 30 hours. During the pour for the first roof section, a heavy thunderstorm washed some of the fresh concrete away. Boxing was improved and a weather watch became a critical part of the process.

The arched hangars are built for permanency, huge and solid, not intended to be bombproof, but designed to be blast and splinter-proof in walls, door panels (each one weighing 27 tons), and sweeping roof. The two hangars were completed at a cost of £76,750 each.

Ohakea hangar under construction, January 1939, showing the arch-forming structure below and scaffolding above for concrete delivery.
(*Evening Post*, 18 January 1939)

Side elevation showing newly formed roof-arch sections, footings (nearest), rear gable and overhead concrete scaffold, January 1939. (National Library, PAColl-5927-05)

Forming structure being moved past the administration building to the site of the second hangar, No. 3. (National Library, PAColl-5927-06)

Ohakea hangar construction, April 1939. Men working on the roof of the first hangar, while footings for the second take shape in the background. (*Northern Advocate*, 24 April 1939)

Whenuapai's two hangars, the second still under construction, 13 September 1940. (Alexander Turnbull Library Ref: WA-21413-G)

The airfield required levelling, drainage (24 miles of pipework) and grassing.[2] In 1940, the *Evening Post* reported:

> There are miles of main and herringbone drainage under the grass surface and their effectiveness has been now well proved by winter rains. At most, while downpours last, the flood pools do not stop flying, and the drainage system carries all surface water off in a few hours.

Meanwhile, a start had already been made on another new base being built to accommodate the second bomber squadron (No. 2 Squadron RNZAF) at Whenuapai, near Auckland. Airfield levelling was underway there by March 1939, however the site chosen meant some delays due to additional design work required for heavier foundations.

The same hangar construction techniques were employed at Whenuapai; the Ohakea fabricated steel concrete-forming structure for the hangars was dismantled, shipped to Auckland and re-used. In early December, a gust of wind caused part of the forming structure to collapse during re-assembly, but no serious damage was done. The two Whenuapai hangars would not be completed until late 1940.

Each bomber base cost almost a million pounds – a huge investment at the time. It is testament to these pioneering designs that, 80 years later, the hangars are still in use.

Construction at Ohakea was expected to be finished just in time for the first flight's arrival in late October. In fact, the station opened for business in September 1939, a month before the Wellingtons were due.

According to press reports of the day, the first 15 Wellingtons to arrive were to be retained by No. 1 Squadron, Ohakea, and the next 15 would go to No. 2 Squadron at Whenuapai. Following RAF practice, 12 aircraft would have been operated by each squadron, with the other six kept as reserve airframes. According to newspaper reports, stocks of bombs and ammunition had been built up 'sufficient for the first twelve months of operations'.

Together with construction work underway at the Hobsonville and Wigram air bases, the full Air Force expansion programme was planned to be completed by 31 December 1940, by which time the last flight of Wellingtons would have arrived.[3]

~ ~ ~ ~ ~ ~ ~ ~

Notes & References

1. Chas. Wm. Turner, M.Eng., B.Sc. (Eng), 'Reinforced Concrete Hangars for Air Force Stations in New Zealand', *New Zealand Institution of Engineers Proceedings*, 1948, Vol. XXXIV.

2. Ohakea would operate as a grass airfield until Japan entered the war in December 1941, after which work would begin on concreting the runways to handle the even larger and heavier aircraft coming into service.

3. Report by the Honourable F. Jones, Minister in Charge of the Air Department, for the Year Ended 31st of March 1939, NZ Government, Appendices to the Journals of House of Representatives (and the Votes & Proceedings), PapersPast, National Library of New Zealand.

The 1st Mobile Flight

'Schedule of Officers and Airmen Crews, 1st New Zealand Mobile Flight
Six Wellington Aircraft Scheduled to Leave United Kingdom 1:10:39.' (Archives New Zealand)

On 15 August 1939, Sid Wallingford signed off on a list of the six crews and their allocated aircraft that would make up the historic first ferry flight, the '1st New Zealand Mobile Flight'.

The five-man crews each included two Royal New Zealand Air Force (RNZAF) officer pilots and three technicians needed to operate and service the aircraft during the trip, and on arrival in New Zealand. Maurice Buckley, with Cyril Kay as lead navigator, would pilot NZ306, leading the first group of three aircraft. Aubrey Breckon (with Trevor Freeman as co-pilot) would lead the others. NZ306 was to be the Air-to-Surface Vessel-equipped aircraft, although Dr Ernest Marsden was not listed as a passenger. Wireless equipment would be installed, and each aircraft was allocated a 'ZM' radio callsign.

These were the second batch of aircraft. The Mark IA was a significant improvement over the Mark I: slightly larger (a bigger bomb bay); more manoeuvrable Nash & Thompson turrets (FN 5 front and FN 10 rear, both twin machine gun); an FN 25 retractable, ventral turret (not always fitted); a revised oxygen system; a better sound-proofed cockpit; standard astrodome; bigger wheels; a new "power egg" compatible engine nacelle, and a strengthened airframe and undercarriage. A fuel-jettison system and flotation bags were now standard, making part of the NZ specification redundant. Possibly for this reason, another change to the order had been made and the RNZAF 'special' requirements were removed, even though production had already begun. The remaining machines were to be built 'as far as possible to RAF standards'. Long-range fuel and oil tanks were ordered separately. Surprisingly, at a provisional price of £13,000.00 each, the Mark IAs were cheaper than their predecessors.

~ ~ ~ ~ ~ ~ ~ ~

Meanwhile, in mid-August, the designated commanding officer of the 2nd Mobile Flight, freshly promoted Squadron Leader Ronald 'Nugget' Cohen RNZAF, arrived at Marham and began training, along with another 2nd Mobile Flight pilot, Flying Officer Ian Morrison RNZAF.

Both were experienced men. Cohen had joined the Royal Air Force (RAF) in 1929 and served in Britain, Iraq and the Middle East. He had returned to New Zealand in 1935, joined the RNZAF and became Chief

Flying Instructor at the Flying Training School at Wigram. Morrison had sailed to England in 1935, joined the RAF in 1936 on a short-service commission and had recently undertaken a special navigation course at Manston.

Another pilot and navigation specialist had been nominated for the 2nd Mobile Flight but not yet posted in. Flying Officer Charlie Clark was a New Zealander flying Hudsons with No. 233 Squadron, based at Leuchars in Scotland.[1]

Back in New Zealand, six more RNZAF technicians had been selected to go to England for training, and the announcement by the Minister of Defence, Mr Fred Jones, suggested they were intended for the 2nd Mobile Flight:[2]

> They will carry out preliminary training with this squadron before acting as wireless operators and mechanics on the flight to New Zealand towards the end of this year.

They were wireless electrical mechanics George Perrott, Frank George, Thomas Smith and Norman Murray, and wireless operators Graham French and Trevor Goodhue. They left Wellington on the passenger liner RMS *Rangitiki* on 29 July, arriving in England exactly a month later, expecting to join the New Zealand Squadron and commence training.

Wireless technicians GH French, N Murray, TJ Goodhue and TG Smith. (2018/9/34/17, Hawke's Bay Museums Trust)

Cohen was due to assemble his 2nd Mobile Flight crews to start training by 1 October, just as the first flight was leaving, at which point he would assume command of the New Zealand Squadron from

Buckley. He would lead the 2nd Mobile Flight when it flew out from England approximately two months later and hand over command to Sidney Wallingford, leader of the 3rd Mobile Flight.[3]

The 3rd Mobile Flight was to form for training on 1 December, and the 4th Mobile Flight on 1 July 1940. The leader of the 4th Flight had already been named (Squadron Leader James Findlay); however, as with Wallingford, events overtook these plans.

No announcements had yet been made regarding personnel for the 5th Mobile Flight but newspaper reports indicated it would probably take place around September or October:

> A great deal of organisation will be behind the dispatch of the Wellingtons to New Zealand. Each of the 30 bombers will have a crew of seven men, which means that at least 210 men will have to take part in a rigorous preparation.[4]

Each Wellington was allocated two pilots, meaning 60 pilots were needed across the five flights. The original plan mentioned 40 RAF pilots being repatriated, so perhaps it envisaged some of the crews from the early flights travelling back to the UK to repeat the trip.

Once the fifth (and last) flight had left, the New Zealand Squadron would be wound up, its members either having flown out to New Zealand to assist in the setup of the two new RNZAF bomber squadrons or returned to service with the RAF. Before the 1st Mobile Flight left, however, the decision was made to record preparations for the historic event, and no doubt generate some newspaper coverage back home.

The Wellingtons were a high-profile component of the government's defence expansion programme and the arrival of the aircraft for the new squadrons would coincide nicely with the New Zealand Government's extensive centenary celebrations planned for 1940. Vickers-Armstrongs had even taken the opportunity to send a model of a Wellington bomber out to New Zealand for display in the Centennial Exhibition. It was also a time when long-distance aviation was still making the news. Two squadrons of the latest bombers were about to be flown halfway around the world, an unprecedented feat requiring considerable organisation, skill and daring.

Sometime in late August 1939, a photographer visited Marham to take a set of publicity photos. Several of these have survived in private photograph albums and copies of some are held in the archives of the Air Force Museum of New Zealand at Wigram, Christchurch.

~ ~ ~ ~ ~ ~ ~ ~

Posing for the camera, New Zealand Squadron pilots examine a map and a bubble sextant. Left to right: S/L Cyril Kay, S/L Maurice Buckley, F/O John Adams, P/O Wilfred Williams, P/O Trevor Freeman (holding sextant), F/O John Collins (leaning over Freeman), F/O Neville Williams and F/O Arthur Greenaway. Wellington NZ304 in the background.
(TO Freeman collection, Air Force Museum of NZ)

F/O John Collins talking to F/O Arthur Greenaway from the cockpit, NZ304 in the background. (Air Force Museum of NZ)
Below, Greenaway and Collins. (MW Buckley collection)

Four New Zealand Squadron Wellingtons Mark I lined up, NZ302 second closest to camera, as a No. 115 Squadron Wellington takes off in the background, RAF Marham, August 1939. (Air Force Museum of NZ)

'Pilots of No. 1 New Zealand Flight.' The original 12 pilots of the New Zealand Squadron's 1st Mobile Flight at RAF Marham in August 1939. Left to right: F/O John Collins, F/L Charles Hunter, F/O John Adams, P/O Trevor Freeman, S/L Cyril Kay, S/L Maurice Buckley, F/O Arthur Greenaway, F/O Aubrey Breckon, P/O Neville Williams, F/O Fred Lucas, P/O William Coleman and P/O Wilfred Williams. (Air Force Museum of NZ)

Members of the New Zealand Squadron's 1st Mobile Flight in front of Wellington NZ302 (serial partially visible under the wing), RAF Marham, August 1939. Front row, left to right: P/O Trevor Freeman, P/O Wilfred Williams, F/O John Adams, F/O John Collins, F/O Arthur Greenaway, F/L Charles Hunter, S/L Maurice Buckley, S/L Cril Kay, F/O Aubrey Breckon, F/O Neville Williams, P/O William Coleman and F/O Fred Lucas.

The rear rank consists of 17 of the other 18 airmen that made up the six original 1st Mobile Flight crews including the six RNZAF specialists named in the crews: LAC Ted Williams (8th from left); Cpl Bill Steven (9th); AC1 Ronald Anderson (10th); Cpl Tom Read (11th); AC1 Don McGlashan (12th) ; AC1 Joe White (far right). Standing at the back are the four RNZAF wireless specialist – Ron Anderson, Don McGlashan, Joe White and Ted Williams – as well as Dick Read and Bill Steven, the two RNZAF fitters. Making up the rest of the back row are the RAF technicians listed in the 1st Mobile Flight crews: (Air Force Museum of NZ)

Another, larger, formal group photo shows what appears to be the full New Zealand Squadron as it was in late August 1939, in front of Wellington NZ302, RAF Marham, August 1939. Front row, left to right: P/O Trevor Freeman, P/O Wilfred Williams, F/O John Adams, F/O John Collins, F/O Arthur Greenaway, F/L Charles Hunter, (possibly) S/L Ronald J Cohen, S/L Maurice Buckley, S/L Cyril Kay, F/O Aubrey Breckon, (possibly) P/O Meyer-Williams RAF (instructor pilot), F/O Neville Williams, P/O William Coleman and F/O Fred Lucas.

Others identifiable: LAC Ted Williams (fifth from left, standing), Cpl Bill Steven (directly behind S/L Cohen), Cpl Donald McGlashan (top rear, above S/L Kay), then, left to right, AC1 Ron Anderson, Cpl Thomas Read, unknown and AC1 Joe White. F/Sgt Edwin Roberts RAF (administrator) is directly behind S/L Buckley. This photo potentially includes three more pilots active with the squadron at the time: Squadron Leader 'Nugget' Cohen RNZAF, already at Marham to start assembling the 2nd Mobile Flight; and two RAF instructors on loan from 38 Squadron, Pilot Officer Meyer-Williams RAF and Sergeant Sach. It also includes RAF ground crew and squadron administration personnel (Appendix 1). (Air Force Museum of New Zealand)

Notes & References

1. 'Air Force Casualty', *Evening Post*, 13 October 1939.
2. 'New Defence Planes', *Otago Daily Times*, 12 July 1939.
3. 'Flight to Dominion', *Manawatu Standard*, 31 July 1939.
4. 'Ahead of Schedule', *Evening Post*, 18 May 1939.

War Intervenes

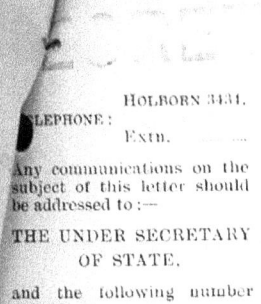

Letter from NZ Liaison Officer S/L Sidney Wallingford to OC New Zealand Squadron S/L Maurice Buckley advising that, in the event of war, the New Zealand Squadron 'is to be placed at the disposal of the Royal Air Force', 28 August 1939. (Archives New Zealand)

During the last week in August 1939, the situation in Europe worsened and it was now clear war was not far away. German troops were moving to the Polish border.

On the 24th, the New Zealand Government placed the Air Force on alert. New Zealand offered to place the Wellingtons and Royal New Zealand Air Force (RNZAF) personnel of the squadron at the disposal of the Royal Air Force (RAF). The British Government gratefully accepted. It was the first material contribution to Britain's war effort by any Commonwealth country, and not insignificant; 30 bombers and 60 men. Wallingford advised Buckley on 28 August.

The governor-general declared a state of emergency on 1 September as news came through that Germany had invaded Poland; on the 2nd, Britain mobilised its Army, Navy and Air Force.

Prime Minister Chamberlain announced a state of war with Germany, at 11:15am on Sunday 3 September, when Hitler failed to respond to a demand he suspend all aggressive action against Poland.

In his autobiography, *The Restless Sky*, 'Cyrus' Kay remembered it as a warm and sunny day. He was at home listening to the wireless when Chamberlain made the historic announcement. Kay immediately drove to RAF Marham to report for duty.

Another listening to Chamberlain's address that morning was wireless mechanic Don McGlashan, sitting in one of the NZ Wellingtons doing a daily inspection, with his Type R1082 wireless receiver tuned in to the BBC. He also remembered that last morning of peace as brilliantly fine and warm. Ironically, it was also the day the second batch of six RNZAF Wellingtons was signed over by Vickers-Armstrongs, ready for collection. Sadly, they would not be going to Marham.

At 11:30 that night, the first air raid warning of the war was sounded. It was a false alarm, but a reminder of how vulnerable England suddenly was, easily within the range of German bombers.

The next day, Wallingford confirmed suspension of the balance of the order for 30 Wellingtons and all associated spares and equipment required for the ferry flights. Buckley's pilots and airmen, who had signed up to fly Wellingtons to New Zealand and who had already started packing gear for the trip, now had to face the prospect of staying in England to fight a war with Germany, for how long nobody knew. In the cases of Buckley, Charles Hunter, Arthur Greenaway and Wilfred 'Bill' Williams, their wives and children were already on their way back to New Zealand in anticipation of the arrival of the 1st Mobile Flight.

The men were keen to stay in England and join the war effort, but they also wanted to stay together. Wallingford recognised this in a letter written two days later, passing on the latest official indication that 'so far as is practicable, personnel should be kept together on the same station, and not attached piecemeal'.

It was the start of a seven-month-long discussion – back and forth between the New Zealand Government, the UK Air Ministry, and RAF Bomber Command – over what to do with the unit, too small to stand alone, unable to be quickly expanded with trained New Zealand personnel, far from combat ready, and yet with significant potential morale-building value, both in New Zealand and Britain.

~ ~ ~ ~ ~ ~ ~ ~

The radar-equipped Wellington was one of the six ready for delivery when war intervened. All the evidence points to this being N2874 (NZ306), the aircraft Buckley and Kay were to have flown out to New Zealand, probably with Dr Marsden on board.

Marsden had settled on a Long Range Air-to-Surface Vessel (LRASV) unit, a sideways-looking radar that required an 18-foot-long array of transmitter aerials (five pairs) on top of the rear fuselage, and 12-foot 'curtain' receiver arrays on the sides. The longer array meant LRASV had a range 2.5 times better than the equivalent forward-looking system; it could detect submarines at 10–15 miles. The aerials along the spine gave the aircraft a 'stickleback' appearance. Years later, New Zealand Squadron wireless specialist Don McGlashan remembered seeing the Wellington in question and the distinctive aerials.[1]

With the cancellation of the ferry flights and diversion of the Wellington order to the RAF, the plan to fly the LRASV-fitted aircraft back to New Zealand was abandoned. A newspaper report in October 1944 stated that 'Britain asked, however to be permitted to retain the aircraft, and New Zealand agreed'.[2]

Marsden left England on 30 August, just days before war was declared. He returned home by sea with his detailed reports and the various pieces of equipment he had managed to acquire in England, stopping off briefly in South Africa and Australia to assist in their efforts to adopt the new technology.[3] He carried some parts with him including an ASV set and three television receivers, and generously left one of the receivers with the Australians. The bulkier equipment was shipped separately:

> Cases fragile apparatus being despatched care Captain Akaroa due Auckland 5th October. Arrange for collection without examination and transfer to Wellington.

By the time he arrived back in Wellington in early October, a government 'RDF Advisory Committee' had already been put together and special courses were being developed to train young graduates to work on radar development and manufacture. Under cover of its radio activities, New Zealand's top-secret radar programme was set up as a unit within the Post & Telegraph Department. Within a year, one of the radar teams had a prototype airborne ASV unit built and installed in an aircraft, ready for trials.

~ ~ ~ ~ ~ ~ ~ ~

In New Zealand, the cancellation of the Wellington order was seen as a generous contribution to Britain's war effort, but it created a huge hole in Ralph Cochrane's national air defence plan – leaving the country without any modern front-line aircraft and without some of the RNZAF's most experienced pilots. It also meant New Zealand would be unable to uphold its early warning reconnaissance commitments across the Pacific.

Despite expansion, the RNZAF was still quite small at the outbreak of the war, with only 91 officers and 665 airmen,[4] with a further 79 officers and 325 airmen in the Territorials and 349 pilots in the Civil Reserve. Over the next 18 months, for its coastal reconnaissance and defence, the country had to rely on nine practically obsolete Vickers Vildebeest single-engine biplane bombers, 20 similarly obsolete Blackburn Baffins, a few Fairey Gordons and Vickers Vincents, and some civil de Havilland biplanes impressed into military service. Two Tasman Empire Airways Limited S.30 Empire flying boats could be co-opted for long-range reconnaissance operations, if required.

Without the Wellingtons, New Zealand also lacked aircraft with the range to reach Singapore, seen as the key to the defence of the Pacific. While Britain was facing up to Germany, and potentially Italy, the ability of the Royal Navy to effectively defend Singapore was in serious doubt and Japan could well take advantage of the situation. But even before the Japanese threat eventuated, the German raider *Orion* arrived in New Zealand waters in June 1940, laying mines off Northland and sinking the trans-Pacific liner *Niagara*. Three more ships were sunk in and around New Zealand waters before the end of the year. The limited capabilities of the RNZAF's available aircraft were immediately exposed.

After the sinking of the liner MS *Rangitane* off East Cape in November 1940 (the ship that delivered the six RNZAF wireless specialists to England in February 1939), new prime minister Peter Fraser asked Britain to provide New Zealand with Lockheed Hudsons for coastal patrol, reminding Winston Churchill of New Zealand's gift of the Wellingtons 14 months earlier:[5]

> We have constantly borne in mind the necessity of taking a large view and of balancing our needs with those elsewhere in the common cause, but we wonder if it is fully realised in the United Kingdom how helpless this Dominion is against attacks from seaward.
>
> ... and it is a plain fact that at present the New Zealand Air Force possess not one single aircraft suitable either for reconnaissance or for attack against a raider at any substantial distance from the shores of New Zealand.

Churchill replied, promising to help, but the Hudsons did not arrive until a year later.

~~~~~~~~

So how well would the Wellingtons have performed in their intended front-line roles for the RNZAF around New Zealand and up into the Pacific?

Although generally thought of as a failure as a day bomber, the Wellington eventually achieved success as a night bomber over continental Europe and was very effective in anti-submarine, anti-shipping and maritime-reconnaissance roles, throughout the war and in all theatres. Later versions of ASV would play a big part in the aircraft's effectiveness.

In hindsight, it seems Cochrane's choice was a good one, and that, assuming the lessons were taken from early European operations, the Wellingtons could have served New Zealand well in defending the country from seaborne threats.

~~~~~~~~

Notes & References

1. David Duxbury, via the Wings Over New Zealand Forum, https://rnzaf.proboards.com/thread/27785/wellingtons-reached-nz-september-1939.

2. 'Churchill's Prophecy When He Saw Radar', *Auckland Star*, 23 October 1944, via Dave Homewood, Wings Over New Zealand Forum, https://rnzaf.proboards.com/thread/28518/zealanders-involved-wwii-science-development.

3. DSIR [Department of Scientific and Industrial Research] World War 2 Narratives. No 3. Radar. Copy No. 3, Reference: AAOQ 28051 W3424 16/, Archives New Zealand.

4. Air Department (report on the), for the Year 1939–40, Appendix to the Journals of the House of Representatives, 1940 Session I, H-37.

5. F.L.W. Wood, *Political and External Affairs, The Official History of New Zealand in the Second World War 1939–1945*, Chapter 16, pp. 213–14.

Taking Stock

Back in England, the six aircraft intended to fly to New Zealand in the 1st Mobile Flight were sitting at Weybridge awaiting their fate, following cancellation of the Royal New Zealand Air Force (RNZAF) order. As Buckley later wrote:[1]

> A later type had been evolved and the first six of these were actually delivered the day War broke out.
>
> Our beautiful new machines had to have their distinctive New Zealand markings erased and were sent to an RAF Squadron who could use them at once against the enemy.

A week after the 4 September cancellation, the six new Wellingtons, NZ306–11, had their Royal Air Force (RAF) serials, N2874–79, reinstated.

By the end of another week, all except N2874 had been allocated to front-line RAF squadrons. When N2874 (the radar-equipped machine) was eventually transferred to the RAF in December 1939, it was not to an operational squadron but to the Aeroplane and Armament Experimental Establishment at Boscombe Down.

The next batch of six Mark IAs, originally intended as NZ312–17, left Weybridge in October, under their RAF serial numbers, N2937–42, and went straight to operational squadrons.

NZ300 remained at Weybridge. It was test flown again at Weybridge by 'Mutt' Summers on the 10th and 13th of July, but still not delivered. Eventually, it was transferred in November to No. 5 Maintenance Unit, RAF Kemble, as a 'reserve aircraft'.

The New Zealand Squadron would have to keep making do with its five Wellington Mark Is.

A few days after the cancellation, Sidney Wallingford amended it in response to Maurice Buckley's concerns it might leave the unit short on spares and equipment needed to continue training at Marham. He reminded Buckley, however, that any future requests for equipment would have to go through the proper RAF channels.

The decision to turn the Wellingtons and crews over to the RAF effectively cancelled plans for recruiting and posting in personnel for the subsequent flights, leaving the unit, for the time being, at less than half-squadron strength. The six wireless specialists who had just arrived in England for the second ferry flight had been posted to No. 99 Squadron, Mildenhall, which operated Wellingtons, on 1 September. They would not be going to Marham.

Meanwhile, with the possibility of air raids and invasion from across the Channel, RAF squadrons were being dispersed to less vulnerable airfields. Some of the New Zealand Squadron's aircraft were moved to Birmingham on 6 September, and then for a few days to Barton Bendish, a bare, damp field five miles south-west of Marham.

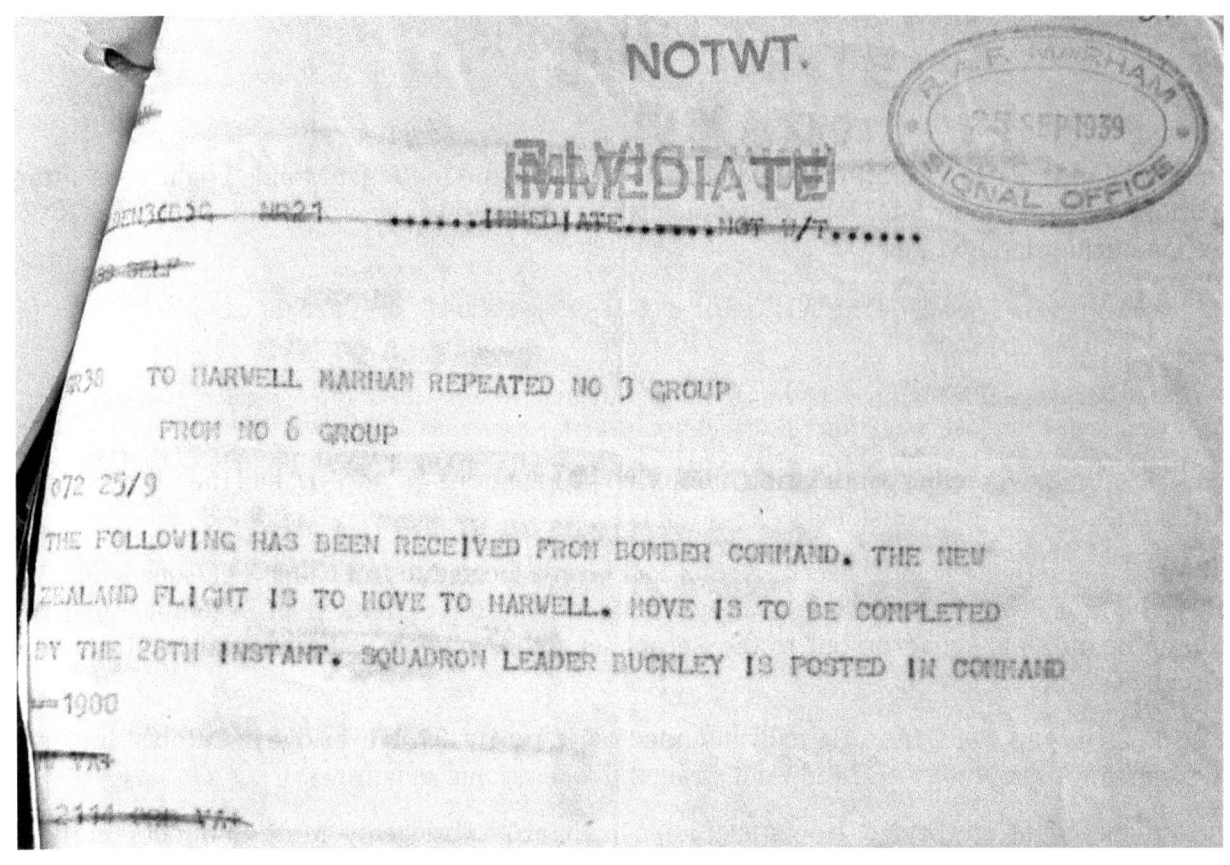

Telegram from 6 Group ordering the New Zealand Flight to move from Marham to Harwell. (Archives New Zealand)

On the 25th, orders were received from No. 6 Group to relocate the entire unit to Harwell, near Oxford, by the 28th.

On the 27th, Buckley, with Aubrey Breckon piloting NZ301 – and 'Popeye' Lucas, Sergeant Mees, Leading Aircraftman Pomeroy and Aircraftman Flegg on board – led the other four Wellingtons on the 45-minute flight across to Harwell. The other pilots were Ronald Cohen, 'Bill' Coleman, John Collins and Charles Hunter. On the 29th, operational training began in earnest at Harwell.

One of Buckley's first jobs was to carry out a 'stocktake' of his assets. The unit was made up of 14 RNZAF officer pilots, six RNZAF technicians and two specialist RAF officers, with the balance being RAF airmen and technicians 'on loan'. Of the 12 pilots assigned to the 1st Flight, Hunter is listed as signals instructor, Greenaway as armament instructor, and Breckon as photographic specialist. The unit had two 'supernumerary' pilots originally intended for the 2nd Mobile Flight, Squadron Leader 'Nugget' Cohen and Flying Officer Ian Morrison. Buckley listed each pilot's experience, flying qualifications, Wellington test status, Wellington flying hours and total flying hours. Two RAF specialists were listed, Squadron Leader Pettit, 'Navigational Instructor for Sqdn', and Flying Officer Frost, squadron engineering officer.

There were the four wireless operators, two wireless mechanics (one of whom was also an air gunner), one instrument repairer, eight fitters, 12 flight riggers, nine flight mechanics, one fitter aero (engines), one electrician, one metal rigger, one equipment assistant and six aircraft hands.

This would have given the squadron a total of 14 pilots, around 50 other ranks, and five aircraft. By comparison, the fully operational, Marham-based No. 38 Squadron had 27 pilots, 210 other ranks airmen and 18 Wellingtons, of which 12 were serviceable for operations.

The RNZAF Wellingtons were not at all operations ready as they had been intended for ferry flight training purposes only. Buckley wrote that to equip them properly 'the compiled list of items required did actually fill two file covers'. NZ301–305 were listed at the end of August as being fitted with 'full flotation gear and jettison gear, overload tanks, front and rear turrets and oxygen attachments. No wireless or guns'. The Wellingtons would definitely need guns!

Despite the New Zealand Government's description of their new aircraft as 'heavily armed', the Mark I's standard armament was only three 0.303-in machine guns: one Vickers K in the front turret and twin Brownings in the rear. The Vickers gun turrets were poorly designed affairs with limited manoeuvrability and inflexible ammunition feeds prone to jamming.[2] The turrets had a hydraulically operated rotating gun mount, but a fixed transparent Perspex cupola (dome-shaped windscreen). The gunner's seat was also fixed, meaning he had to twist his body as the gun rotated, making it difficult to traverse, let alone sight, through 180 degrees.

Up until now, NZ301–5 had been coded 'B'–'F', the missing identification code 'A' presumably having been reserved for the undelivered NZ300. At Harwell, they were re-coded 'A'–'E'.

A memo from Buckley dated 29 September listed personnel requirements to bring the unit up to operational strength as 12 pilots, six air observers, 18 wireless operators and 14 armourers. He suggested the six New Zealand wireless operators at Mildenhall be posted in as originally intended, to no avail. In a second memo dated 18 October, he presented a timetable for the arrival of trainee personnel and 12 new Wellingtons to achieve a full-strength, 'operationally fit' squadron by 31 January 1940.

Flight Lieutenant Wilfred Collett, a New Zealander with 38 Squadron, joined them briefly at Harwell. Collett flew 16 times with the squadron during October 1939, initially dual training and practice flights with S/L Buckley as captain and instructor. However, he disappears from the Flight Authorisation Book at the end of the month, so presumably he was 'on loan', or temporarily attached. Collett would return to the squadron seven months later as a flight commander.

The key figure in Buckley's efforts to scrape together equipment and consumables to keep the unit functioning was Flight Sergeant Edwin Roberts, described in *Return at Dawn* (the first official history of the squadron) as Buckley's 'Admirable Crichton':

> The position was unique in the Royal Air Force. Everything from a windscreen wiper to a Bristol Pegasus XVIII nine-cylinder air-cooled radial engine, from a blotting-pad to a Remington, had to be obtained and, what is more, paid for by the New Zealand Government. They were obtained.

Roberts ran the squadron's administration, wrote letters, filled in forms, kept records 'and generally became the jack of all branches'. His office doubled as the pilots' mess; Buckley talks of games of darts being played while Roberts carried out his paperwork.[3]

At the same time, RNZAF Sergeants Bill Steven and Thomas Read ran the engineering and maintenance programmes, and the four RNZAF wireless specialists – Anderson, McGlashan, White and Williams – also played important roles in keeping the unit's aircraft in the air.

Training was now deadly serious; however, the colonials brought with them a more casual, pragmatic attitude that didn't always sit comfortably in the RAF. An insight into the culture is given in a story told by Leading Aircraftman Dick Smith,[4] an RAF fitter who emigrated to New Zealand after the war:

> My story concerns Cpl Joe White. As we passed the guardroom, off-duty, Joe tucked his cap into his belt. Suddenly a SP [Service Police] Corporal ran out of the guardroom and yelled 'Corporal, put your cap on!'

Joe yelled back 'I didn't travel 12,000 ******* miles to help fight a ******* war to put my cap on, so get stuffed!' The shocked SP retreated into his kennel. This made my day as ordinary airmen had to put up with a lot of 'bull' in those days.

On 9 November 'Popeye' Lucas and Bill Coleman took two Wellingtons up for an hour of "photos" and gun turret practice around Harwell, a photographer on board NZ304 capturing rare aerial shots of NZ302 over the English countryside.

~ ~ ~ ~ ~ ~ ~ ~

Wellington NZ302 flown by 'Popeye' Lucas near Harwell, 9 November 1939. (Above, F.J. Lucas collection; below, A.A.N. Breckon collection, Air Force Museum of NZ)

Notes & References

1. Suggested script for Group Captain Buckley's Broadcast to New Zealand, letter to H.L. Saunders, Air Ministry, 20 August 1941, M.W. Buckley collection.

2. Ken Delve, *Vickers-Armstrongs Wellington*, The Crowood Press Ltd, Wiltshire, 1998, p.14.

3. Personal narrative, M.W. Buckley collection.

4. 'An Erk on 75 Squadron', *Bomber Command Assn (NZ) newsletter*, No. 44, June 1996.

Nobody's Children

During their time at Harwell it began to look as though the New Zealand Squadron might be broken up and its members posted to different Wellington squadrons.

Maurice Buckley was insistent the unit be kept intact, along with its New Zealand identity, lobbying and receiving crucial support from the Air Officer Commanding, No. 3 Group, Air Vice-Marshal Jack Baldwin CB OBE DSO, and Air Officer Commanding-in-Chief, Bomber Command, Air Chief Marshal Sir Edgar Ludlow-Hewitt KCB CMG DSO MC. Baldwin requested that, if it was not possible to form a 'Dominion Squadron' around them, they be posted to an existing squadron as a 'Dominion Flight'. However, once these recommendations had been made, the decision was in the hands of the New Zealand Government.

The politicians in Wellington agreed in principle but indicated, for the time being, New Zealand would not be able to provide the necessary aircrew and maintenance personnel for a full squadron due to its own training scheme expansion commitments. It was suggested the proposal should be discussed at an upcoming conference in Canada, and that what was now increasingly referred to as 'the New Zealand Flight' 'should proceed with existing training programme as speedily as possible'.[1]

Another unknown was how Royal New Zealand Air Force (RNZAF) personnel would operate within the Royal Air Force (RAF), conditions (including pay) differing significantly. For example, while serving in the UK in late 1939, with special allowances, Squadron Leader Cyril Kay was paid £1,012 per annum, whereas serving in the RAF he would have been earning £803. Flight Lieutenant Aubrey Breckon was paid £762, compared to the RAF equivalent pay of £521; Pilot Officer 'Bill' Coleman £522 versus £389.

Most of the pilot officers had held short-service commissions (SSCs) in the RAF. New Zealand Liaison Officer (NZLO) Sid Wallingford had prepared 'agreements' covering their transfers to five-year commissions in the RNZAF and sent these to Buckley on 23 August for signing. But now they were staying in England, facing the prospect of serving as members of the RNZAF within the RAF, potentially dispersed among different squadrons, several officers refused to sign their agreements. Concerns appear to have been around loss of seniority and opportunities that had previously been available to them in their hard-won RAF careers.

Wallingford grumbled about the non-signings in a letter to Buckley on 19 September, suggesting the RAF may not honour their SSCs should the war end quickly, and that they may have already lost their previous seniority. He warned 'If the agreements are not signed there is a risk that they will become "nobody's children" with all the consequences.' Five of the officers (Breckon, Coleman, John Collins, Fred Lucas and Neville Williams) held out and in fact took the extra step of lodging applications to transfer back to the RAF.

This situation festered for another four months, letters sent back and forth between the Air Ministry, the NZLO and Buckley, attempting to dissuade them. Eventually, the Air Ministry imposed a set of quite harsh conditions on any transfer back to the RAF:

- refund all Air Ministry gratuities received during time with the RNZAF

- time with the RNZAF to be treated as leave without pay

- applicants cannot be posted to their old units

- applicants would not be eligible for re-transfer to the RNZAF during hostilities

It was not until February 1940 that the situation was resolved[2] when, 'owing to the severe conditions imposed', the five finally withdrew their applications and accepted they would be staying with the RNZAF.

Meanwhile, Buckley's promotion to wing commander had been gazetted on 1 November 1939, recognition that his responsibilities were now more than just the command of a flight. Some confusion has surrounded the name of the unit, from its establishment until achieving full squadron status, often being referred to down the years as 'the New Zealand Flight'.

While the official parent unit was clearly the New Zealand Squadron, set up to oversee the formation and training of a series of six ferry (Mobile) flights, only one ferry flight was ever formed. It was variously referred to as the '1st New Zealand Mobile Flight', 'No. 1 (N.Z.) Flight', '1st Flight', '1st Wellington Flight' and, more commonly as time went by, 'the New Zealand Flight'.

As Wallingford said in January 1940, 'the New Zealand Squadron which existed at Marham prior to the outbreak of hostilities cannot be considered a squadron as defined in the R.A.F'. He went on to say, 'the unit which is now termed the New Zealand Flight has continued to train with these aircraft at Harwell'.

It made more sense now to refer to the unit as a flight because it was well below the strength of an operational squadron and needed significant building up to reach that level. The term 'flight' was used commonly in high-level communications through this transitional period, right up to the levels of the Air Ministry, the Chief of the Air Staff and New Zealand's Prime Minister.[3]

On 13 November, Buckley received a boost in manpower, a major step towards full squadron strength. Seventeen RAF wireless operator/air gunners were posted into Harwell for the New Zealand Squadron,[4] all with the rank of Aircraftman 2nd Class (AC2): Gilbert Adams, Eric Albert, John 'Stan' Brooks, 'Reg' Day, John Dowds, Humphrey Edwards, Sidney Garrard, John Gibb, Jack Gibbs, Frank Green, Ian Hamilton, Herbert Kitson, John Murphy, Frank Read, Bernard Shuttleworth, Harold Smith and Lewis White.

At the same time, seven new RAF observers arrived: Sergeants William Allinson, Norman Brown, Jim Carter, Robert Ellis, Robert Hughes, Donald Mackay and George Thorpe.

On 14 November, the unit's five Wellingtons officially reverted to their original RAF serial numbers:

NZ301 ('A') became L4330

NZ302 ('B') – L4340

NZ303 ('C') – L4350

NZ304 ('D') – L4355

NZ305 ('E') – L4360

The new Form 78 cards issued reflected the uncertainty of the situation, with Reason for Allotment recorded as 'Training of crews for Wellington Squadrons of No. 3 (B) Group'.

RAF Aircraft Movement Card for Wellington I, serial number L4330 (previously NZ301).
Initially allocated to 'RAF Harwell for NZ Flight'. (Bomber Command History)

At the end of the month, two new pilots arrived: Pilot Officer Donald Harkness and Flying Officer Samuel Watson. Both were New Zealanders serving in the RAF. Another New Zealand pilot in the RAF, Pilot Officer Richard Hogg, arrived mid-December.

Early in December, Peter Fraser, New Zealand's deputy prime minister, was in London and, at a meeting to discuss the formation of a New Zealand Squadron,[5] it was suggested by the Air Ministry that if sufficient New Zealand personnel were not immediately available, the full complement could be made up by the RAF. Fraser agreed to discuss this suggestion with his colleagues and the New Zealand Air Staff on his return.

On the 16th, Buckley posted a memo 'Aircraft Crews for Training' listing six 'crews' of three aircraftman (AC) wireless operator/air gunners each.

Training took into account the harsh lessons Bomber Command was learning from its early encounters with the *Luftwaffe*. The Wellington was Britain's most advanced bomber, envisaged as an unescorted day bomber capable of defending itself from enemy fighters with the combined firepower of multiple aircraft flying in formation. However, this theory was challenged right from the second day of the war, when two Wellingtons and five Blenheims were lost to anti-aircraft fire and fighters defending German warships in the Schillig Roads. It was then shattered by what became known as 'The Battle of Heligoland Bight'.

```
                AIRCRAFT CREWS FOR TRAINING.
                                                            16/12/39

            The following will operate as crews until further
                              notice.


        No.1.       1st. W/T AG.        2nd. WTAG.         3rd. WTAG.

                    A.C. Edwards.       A.C. White.        A.C. Dowds.

         " 2.       A.C. Green.         A.C. Gibbs.        A.C. Hamilton.

         " 3.       A.C. Smith.         A.C. Albert.       A.C. Brooks.

         " 4.       A.C. Kitson.        A.C. Murphy.       A.C. Shuttleworth.

         " 5.       A.C. Gibb.          A.C. Read.         A.C. Day.

         " 6.       A.C. Garrard.       A.C. Adams.


                                        Wing Commander
                                        Officer Commanding
                                        New Zealand Squadron.
```

'Aircraft Crews for Training', New Zealand Squadron, 16 December 1939. (Archives New Zealand)

On 14 December, 12 Wellingtons from No. 99 Squadron, led by Squadron Leader Andrew 'Square' McKee, a New Zealander, were involved in another attack on a German convoy in the Schillig Roads north of Wilhelmshaven. A combination of early warning by German radar, anti-aircraft fire and large numbers of fighters resulted in five Wellingtons being shot down, for the loss of one enemy fighter and no damage inflicted on any ships. Corporal Colin 'Tod' Knight, one of the original six RNZAF wireless specialists sent to England to train for the Wellington ferry flights, was flying in the lead aircraft that day as wireless operator in McKee's crew:[6]

> I can still see the tracer flying around the aircraft as I was sending the sighting report and, when we got back, to find petrol pouring out of punctured tanks! I saw aircraft of our squadron with wings blazing, falling out of the sky.

Another Wellington that had been damaged in the battle crashed when attempting to land back at Newmarket, killing three of the crew.

Then, on 18 December, a force of 24 Wellingtons from Nos. 9, 37 and 149 Squadrons attacked German naval ships near Wilhelmshaven. This time they bombed from 13,000 feet to try to reduce the effectiveness of the anti-aircraft defences, but again the formations were broken up and German radar-directed fighters got among the Wellingtons. Twelve were shot down and 56 airmen lost for the loss of

The three RAF wireless operators in Crew No. 3, ACs 'Smudge' Smith, 'Stan' Brooks and Eric Albert. (NZ Bomber Command Assn., Stan Brooks collection, via Anna Rhodes-Sayer)

two German fighters. By shocking coincidence, three of the 9 Squadron Wellingtons shot down that day were originally intended for delivery to the RNZAF and the 2nd Mobile Flight.

Losses of 50% were staggering and an unacceptable outcome that eventually led to a complete revision of Bomber Command tactics, the Wellington being moved to primarily night operations. It was a serious setback for the RAF, immediately reducing the effectiveness of its bomber force and forcing a complete change in approach.

These early daylight operations also highlighted deficiencies in the traverse of the Vickers turrets, the ineffectiveness of the ventral 'dustbin' turret against beam attack from above and the fire danger represented by the Wellington's metal fuel tanks which needed to be urgently replaced by the rubber self-sealing type.

The New Zealand Squadron enjoyed Christmas at Harwell and the fateful year ended with Buckley's unit training hard, but still a long way short of his goal to be at full strength and 'operationally fit' by 31 January 1940. At least by now it seemed fairly certain the unit was going to be kept together and built into a full squadron.

Pilot Officer Alfred Charles, an RAF 'Commissioned Air Gunner' arrived in early January to take up the role of gunnery officer.

But it must have felt like a case of 'two steps forward, one back' when, on 12 January, Buckley received advice from the assistant liaison officer, Squadron Leader Fred Newell, that Squadron Leader 'Nugget' Cohen and Flight Lieutenants Arthur Greenaway and Ian Morrison had all been called back to New Zealand by RNZAF Headquarters. They left the squadron shortly afterwards and sailed for home in early February.

Buckley lost another pilot that month when Flight Lieutenant Charles Hunter was also called back, after completing a course at Staff College, Andover. Shortly afterwards, he received advice that Squadron Leader Cyril Kay may also be called back before the end of the year.

~ ~ ~ ~ ~ ~ ~ ~

Notes & References

1. Secret Cypher Telegram from the UK High Commissioner in New Zealand, 3 October 1939.

2. Transfer of R.N.Z.A.F. Officers to Royal Air Force, letter from W/C Buckley to NZLO, Air Ministry, London, 9 February 1940, Archives New Zealand, M.W. Buckley collection.

3. When war broke out in September 1939, Prime Minister Michael Joseph Savage had been seriously ill for some time and Deputy Prime Minister Peter Fraser was already carrying out most of his responsibilities. Savage died on 25 March 1940 and Fraser became prime minister.

4. Telegram from HQ No. 3 Group, 13 November 1939, Archives New Zealand, M.W. Buckley collection.

5. Proposal for Formation of a New Zealand Squadron in the Royal Air Force, minutes of a Meeting held at the Air Ministry (Adastral) House on Saturday 2nd December 1939 at 10.35pm, Buckley collection, Archives New Zealand.

6. *Wimpy: A Detailed Illustrated History of the Vickers Wellington in Service, 1938-1953,* by Steve Bond, Grub Street, 2014, p.37.

Building a Squadron

On 15 January 1940, The New Zealand Squadron moved from Harwell to RAF Stradishall, to come under the command of Air Vice-Marshal Baldwin's No. 3 Group, Bomber Command.

Copies of 'Movement Order No. 2', dated 8 January, were kept by Maurice Buckley, so full instructions have survived, including personnel lists for parties travelling by air, lorries (7), coach and private cars, as well as a full nominal roll. This consisted of 46 pilots and other aircrew, and the same number of ground staff. The aircraft were flown across on 16, 17 and 18 January.

With the old Mark I 'Wimpys' getting tired and now undeniably obsolete, there would have been great excitement on the morning of 25 January when Breckon and Lucas took off in L4350, with no less than eight pilots on board, to bring back four brand-new Wellington Mark IAs from Vickers at Weybridge.[2] The first four collected were P9205, P9206, P9207 and P9209. That afternoon, P9210 and P9212 were also flown across. The six new aircraft were coded as the new 'A'–'F'.

On arrival at Stradishall, four of the old Mark Is – L4330, L4350, L4355 and L4360 – were transferred (on paper) to RAF Stradishall. Apart from L4355, they would see virtually no further use.

In what came to be known as the '1940 Ice Storm', January was the coldest in almost 50 years and, frustratingly, the weather put a stop to flying training. Stradishall's aerodrome was unusable for the first nine days of February. However, it probably offered a welcome break from the relentless routine.

Around this time, two more Royal Air Force (RAF) wireless operator/air gunners arrived – Sgt William Nevill and AC Thomas Mumby.

Training resumed on the 10th, and then, on the 12th, the unit moved from Stradishall to RAF Feltwell.

Air Vice-Marshal Baldwin wanted to move the expanding No. 214 Squadron from Feltwell's satellite station, Methwold, to Stradishall's better facilities to take the load off Methwold's grass airfield in the difficult months of winter and early spring. He also saw benefits in locating the fledgling New Zealand Squadron at Feltwell alongside an experienced operational Wellington unit, No. 37 Squadron.[1] Feltwell would be the unit's home for the next two-and-a-half years.

Two days later, Buckley posted his crew lists, drawn up into 'A' and 'B' Flights.

Training included formation flying practice, searchlight co-operation, low-level bombing and air firing at Berners Heath or over The Wash.

The old Wellingtons were not flown across to Feltwell in the initial move from Stradishall, but L4355 was collected on 16 February, with L4330, L4350 and L4360 following on 1 March.

On 6 March, three of them – L4330 (NZ301), L4360 (NZ305) and L4350 (NZ303) – were transferred out of the squadron (see Appendix 4). Neville and 'Bill' Williams flew L4350 and John Adams and Trevor Freeman took L4360 on the two-hour delivery flight up to No. 22 Maintenance Unit at Silloth, Cumbria, travelling via Northampton and York. John Collins and 'Bill' Coleman brought the four pilots back that afternoon in P9209. L4330 does not appear to have been taken across to Feltwell, so it must have been flown to Silloth direct from Stradishall the same day. That left two of the old Mark I aircraft on strength: L4340 (NZ302) and L4355 (NZ304).

14/2/40

CREWS FOR PRACTICE PURPOSES ONLY.

PROVISIONAL LIST OF AIR CREWS.

"A" FLIGHT		"B" FLIGHT	
S/L KAY	(LEADER)	F/L BRECKON	(LEADER)
P/O FREEMAN.		F/O LUCAS	
SGT CARTER	(NAV:)	SGT HUGHES	(NAV)
L.A.C. ANDERSON	(W/T)	L.A.C. WILLIAMS	(W/T)
A.C. ADAMS	(Front A.G.)	A.C. ALBERT	(Front A.G.)
A.C. Neville	(Rear A.G.)	A.C. MUNBY	(Rear A.G.)

No 2

F/O COLLINS		F/O ADAMS	
P/O HARKNESS		F/O COLEMAN	
SGT THORPE	(NAV)	SGT ALLINSON	(NAV)
A.C. GREEN	(W/T)	A.C. KITSON	(W/T)
A.C. BROOKS	(Front A.G.)	A.C. DAY	(Front A.G.)
A.C. Gibb.	(Rear A.G.)	A.C. GIBBS.	(Rear A.G.)

No 3

P/O WILLIAMS		F/O WILLIAMS	
F/O WATSON		P/O HOGG	
SGT ELLIS	(NAV)	SGT MACKAY	(NAV)
A.C. GARRARD	(W/T)	A.C. SMITH	(W/T)
A.C. MURPHY	(Front A.G.)	A.C. WHITE	(Front A.G.)
A.C. READ	(Rear A.G.)	A.C. HAMILTON	(Rear A.G.)

RESERVES.

SGT BROWN NAV
A.C. EDWARDS. W/T
 "   SHUTTLEWORTH Front A.G.
 "   DOWDS Rear A.G.

Wing Commander
Commanding
New Zealand Squadron.

'Crews for Practice Purposes Only', New Zealand Squadron, Feltwell, dated 14 February 1940. (Archives New Zealand)

LAC Joe White RNZAF, Stradishall, January 1940. (NZ Bomber Command Assn., Stan Brooks collection, via Anna Rhodes-Sayer)

Around this time, the Reverend Arthur Kayll was appointed squadron padre, the only New Zealander to hold that position in the RAF. He came from Waihi and held the rank of squadron leader but was known to all ranks as 'The Padre'. One of his first projects was to obtain a church for the station, again something unique in the RAF, and this he did with the help of prefabricated building manufacturer Boulton & Paul of Norwich, who loaned the building to the squadron for the duration and also provided workmen and materials to set it up. St. George's Church would be finished and dedicated on 7 July, in time for the visit to the station by King George VI on the 19th.

It was also around this time that Buckley had to ground two of his most skilled wireless specialists, Don McGlashan and Joe White. An order from the Air Ministry advised that too many wireless operator mechanics were being lost on operations and they were running out!

Two more New Zealand pilots serving in the RAF arrived on 1 March. Pilot Officers Ian Gow and Geordie Larney were immediately thrown into training.

This was also the day the New Zealand Government officially approved the formation of a New Zealand Squadron within the Royal Air Force; it was not to be a Royal New Zealand Air Force (RNZAF) squadron, but a squadron manned by members of the RNZAF within, and under the command of, the RAF. The various secret cypher telegrams sent that day advising of the decision (including one from the New Zealand governor-general and signed by the prime minister), explained New Zealand's inability to immediately provide personnel from New Zealand, but stated the new squadron should be manned as far as possible by New Zealanders.

What was described cold bloodedly as aircrew 'wastage' was to be met by New Zealanders graduating from the new Empire Air Training Scheme (also known as the British Commonwealth Air Training Plan). Maintenance personnel would be supplied from New Zealand once training expansion requirements had been met. The intention was for RNZAF airmen and technicians to eventually replace all RAF personnel. References in the telegrams to 'the New Zealand Flight, Harwell' highlight the drawn-out decision-making process!

It was assumed 'the cost of the unit will be borne entirely by the RAF', however, differences in RNZAF and RAF pay rates were to be topped up by the New Zealand Government.

~ ~ ~ ~ ~ ~ ~ ~

Notes & References

1. Letter from AVM Baldwin to SASO, SOA 3 Group, 7 February 1940, M.W. Buckley collection, Archives New Zealand.

2. New Zealand Squadron Flight Authorisation Book, Air Force Museum of New Zealand.

COPY OF TELEGRAM   SECRET

FROM   THE GOVERNOR GENERAL OF NEW ZEALAND
TO   THE SECRETARY OF STATE FOR DOMINION AFFAIRS
DATED   1st March 1940

SECRET NO.   His Majesty's Government in New Zealand have had under consideration the question first raised in your telegram of the 27th September, 1939, to the High Commissioner for the United Kingdom in New Zealand, of expanding the New Zealand Flight at MARWELL into a full Squadron by providing personnel to fill the establishment from New Zealand. At that time, and quite irrespective of the Empire Air Training Scheme proposals, it was not possible to provide the personnel from New Zealand without seriously delaying the expansion of the War Training Organisation in New Zealand.

The position at the moment is much the same and until the expansion of the War Training Organisation has been completed at the end of this year it will not be possible to provide any personnel from New Zealand. There are, however, a large number of New Zealand pilots serving in the Royal Air Force, from which to select sufficient pilots for a New Zealand Squadron. New Zealand observers and air gunners will also be available at an early date for posting to this Unit.

His Majesty's Government in New Zealand, therefore agrees to the proposal to expand the New Zealand Flight into a full Squadron to be manned as far as possible by New Zealanders serving in the Royal Air Force. It is suggested that air crew wastage should be met from New Zealanders trained under the Empire Air Training Scheme and that for the time being maintenance personnel should be provided from the Royal Air Force sources. It is also suggested that the Squadron should be equipped with "WELLINGTON" aircraft, the type with which the first Regular Squadron in New Zealand was to be equipped.

It is assumed that the cost of this unit will be borne entirely by the Royal Air Force.

When the full requirements of the War Training Organisation in New Zealand have been met, it is suggested that maintenance personnel should be trained for the Royal Air Force in accordance with the recommendation contained in the Defence Conference Report, Part I, Paragraph 96. Personnel so trained could then replace Royal Air Force personnel in the New Zealand Squadron and thus, in due course it would be possible for the unit to be manned entirely by New Zealanders.

His Majesty's Government in New Zealand would be glad of the views of His Majesty's Government in the United Kingdom on the above proposals.

(SIGNED)   GOVERNOR GENERAL OF NEW ZEALAND

APPROVED
Sgd. P. Fraser.
PRIME MINISTER
/3/1940.

Secret telegram dated 1 March 1940, from the New Zealand governor-general to the Secretary, State Dominion Affairs, confirming the expansion of the New Zealand Flight into a full squadron within the RAF. (Archives New Zealand)

The First Operations

Meanwhile, the squadron-to-be was not waiting around for the paperwork to be completed; the airmen were ready to carry out their first operational sorties of the war.

Despite the losses of December, Bomber Command continued to send aircraft out in daylight to search for and, if possible, attack German shipping in the North Sea. While some sorties were recorded as 'training sweeps', they would have served a useful reconnaissance function, and no doubt would have involved shooting if enemy aircraft had been encountered.

On 10 March 1940, at 1:50pm, two Wellingtons – P9207 'C' captained by Squadron Leader Cyril Kay and P9212 'F' captained by Flying Officer John Collins – took off from Feltwell on the New Zealand Squadron's first wartime operation, a 'Special Sweep':

> **10/03/1940 – <u>Operational</u>.**
> **Two Aircraft carried out Operational Exercise No. 1. Special Sweep, as ordered**
>
> Wellington IA P9207 'C'
>
> S/L Cyril Eyton 'Cyrus' Kay OBE RNZAF – Captain & Pilot
> P/O Trevor Owen Freeman RNZAF NZ1026 – 2nd Pilot
> Sgt Jim Whitlaw Carter RAFVR 527740 – Navigator
> LAC Ronald Alexander John Anderson RNZAF NZ36139 – Wireless Operator
> AC Gilbert Ernest Adams RAF 632805 – Front Gunner
> AC William Eric Nevill RAFVR 631165 – Rear Gunner
>
> Take Off: 1:50 – Landed: 4:05
> Flight Time: 02:15
>
> Wellington IA P9212 'F'
>
> F/O John Noel Collins RNZAF NZ2513 – Captain & Pilot
> P/O Donald Joseph Harkness RAF 41694 – 2nd Pilot
> Sgt George Thorpe RAFVR 523426 – Navigator
> AC Francis William Green RAFVR 581283 – Wireless Operator
> AC John Stanley 'Stan' Brooks, RAFVR 622115 – Front Gunner
> AC John Webster Gibb, RAF 632040 – Rear Gunner
>
> Take Off: 1:50 – Landed: 4:00
> Flight Time: 02:10

For some reason, this historic operation is only partially recorded in the squadron's Operations Record Book (ORB). A very brief description is given in the RAF Form 540 (the wording in bold above) but there is no corresponding entry in the RAF Form 541 'Detail of Work Carried Out'. It should have been the very first entry.[1] Luckily, Maurice Buckley kept hand-written reports of these early operational flights.

The two aircraft flew together to a designated point in the North Sea, then flew back separately so they could practice navigation and wireless procedure over the sea.

> Good landfalls were made by each aircraft and it was felt that as the weather was by no means good, excellent experience was gained by each crew.

Each crew reported having seen several convoys ships, etc. and were able to correctly mark them down.[2]

Flying Officer Collins landed safely back at Feltwell at 4:00pm and Squadron Leader Kay landed five minutes after him.

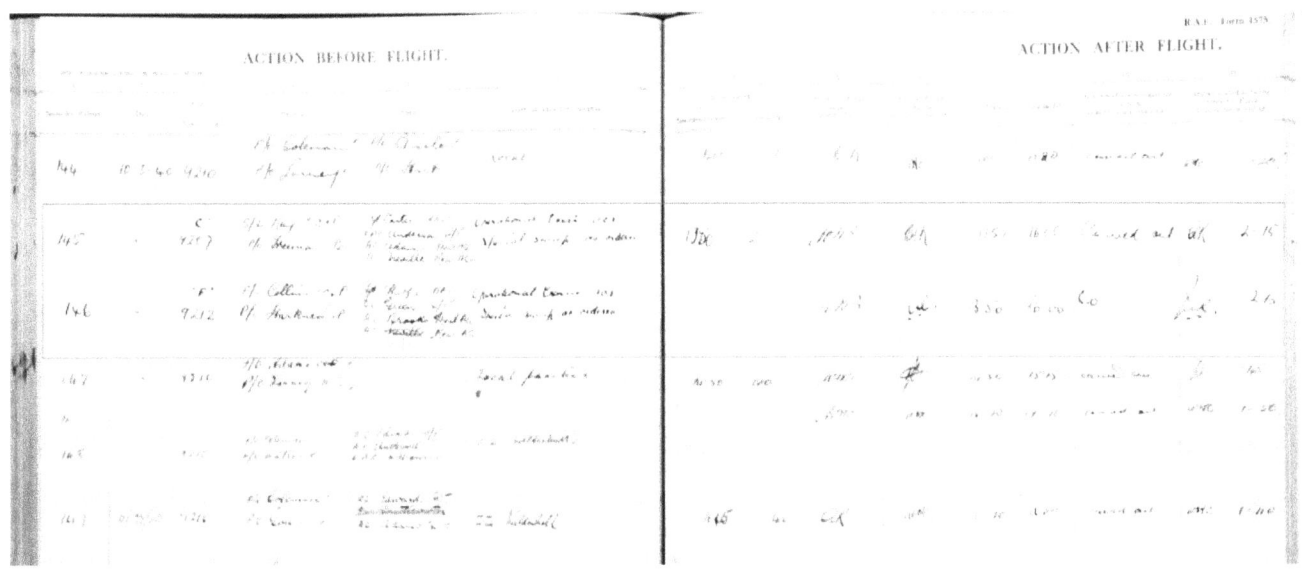

Entries in the New Zealand Squadron Flight Authorisation Book for Operational Exercise No. 1 (highlighted), 10 March 1940. (Air Force Museum of NZ)

Three days later, on 13 March, the same two Wellingtons, P9207 and P9212, this time captained by Flight Lieutenant Aubrey Breckon and Flying Officer 'Jack' Adams respectively, took off from Feltwell on another afternoon Special Sweep over the North Sea. It was the unit's second wartime operation.

13/03/1940 – <u>Operational</u>.
Two Aircraft carried out Operational Exercise No. 1. Special Sweep, as ordered

Wellington IA P9207 'C'

F/L Aubrey Arthur Ninnis Breckon RNZAF NZ1025 – Captain & Pilot
F/O Frederick John 'Popeye' Lucas RNZAF NZ1056 – 2nd Pilot
Sgt Robert Henry Hughes RAF 550880 – Navigator
LAC Edwin Peter 'Ted' Williams RNZAF NZ38235 – Wireless Operator
AC Eric Norman Albert RAF 623339 – Front Gunner
AC Thomas Leonard Mumby RAF 624569 – Rear Gunner

Take Off: 1:55 – Landed: 4:20
Flight Time: 02:25

Operational Flights. New Zealand Squadron.

No 1. Date: 10th March 1940.

Special Sweep over area of North Sea.

Aircraft engaged: Wellington 1A. P.9207. S/L Kay. Captain
P/O Freeman. Pilot.
Sgt Carter. Navigator
L.A.C. Anderson Wireless Operator
A.C. Adams. Front Air Gunner
A.C. Neville Rear Air Gunner

" " " " P.9212. F/O Collins Captain
P/O Harkness Pilot
Sgt Thorpe Navigator
AC Green Wireless Operator
AC Brooks Front Air Gunner
AC Gibb Rear Air Gunner.

Flying Times:- P.9207. 2 hrs 15 mins.
P.9212. 2 hrs 10 mins.

The two aircraft proceeded in company to a point in the North Sea, where they separated and returned seperately.

This gave each aircrew a chance to practice navigation & wireless on the return journey. Good landfalls were made by each aircraft and it was felt that as the weather was by no means good, excellent experience was gained by each crew.

Each crew reported having seen several convoys ships etc. and were able to correctly mark them down.

Operational Report for Operational Flight No. 1, 10 March 1940 (hand-written by Maurice Buckley), Special Sweep over area of North Sea. (M.W. Buckley collection)

Wellington IA P9212 'F'

F/O John 'Jack' Adams RNZAF NZ1027 – Captain & Pilot
P/O Geordie Keith Larney RAF 33582 – 2nd Pilot
Sgt William Alfred Allinson RAF 526281 – Navigator
AC Herbert James Hawkins 'Bert' Kitson, RAF 625948 – Wireless Operator
AC Douglas Reginald 'Reg' Day RAFVR 632887 – Front Gunner
AC Jack Gibbs, RAFVR 625697 – Rear Gunner

Take Off: 1:55 – Landed: 4:15
Flight Time: 02:20

This second operation is the first entered in the squadron's ORB Form 541, recording aircraft, crew members, time up and time down, and captain's comments under 'Details of Sortie or Flight'.

The two aircraft took off at 1:55pm, heading out to the North Sea over Happisburgh, Norfolk, with low cloud soon forcing them to operate separately. A convoy and other ships were seen, photographs were taken, and Adams was challenged by two destroyers, answering with the correct letter of the day. The crews flew home in low cloud and heavy rain, coming in over Wells and landing at Feltwell at 4:20 and 4:15pm respectively.

> The navigation was good and together with the W/T procedure practiced was a very useful exercise.

No doubt relieved at finally getting to contribute to this war, Fred Lucas placed a circled number '1' alongside the entry in his logbook.[3]

A third operation took place on 15 March: 'Operational exercise, Special Sweep, as detailed in No.3 Group Operational Order No.7, dated 14.3.40'. This time aircraft from six No. 3 Group squadrons took part (9, 99, 37, 38, 149 and NZ), the target of their search being a British destroyer. Three aircraft from each squadron were to fly on parallel courses about ten miles apart until a 'sighting' was made.

In the event, the NZ Squadron was only able to put up two aircraft, the same two Wellingtons again, with John Collins captaining P9207 'C' and Jack Adams in P9212 'F'. The two crews took off at 10:30am with Collins leading.

Collins requested a wireless fix at 11:35 which, incredibly, didn't eventuate until 12:50! Not only that, but there was an error in the coordinates provided, which meant they missed the destroyer they were looking for. Little other activity was observed 'other than numerous friendly aircraft and a few ships', so they came back in over Holme-Next-The-Sea and returned safely to base at 2:40pm. Not surprisingly, the operation was described as 'only partly successful'.

A planned operation on the 17th was cancelled but a fourth Special Sweep took place on the 19th. This time Flying Officers 'Bill' Coleman and Neville Williams were flying the 'regular' Wellingtons, with Pilot Officer 'Bill' Williams and crew in P9209 a late cancellation. Both aircraft were airborne at 10:30am, with Coleman landing back at base at 12:35pm; Williams was ten minutes behind him. Both reported minor technical faults: Coleman reported an unserviceable tail wheel light; Williams lost his flap and wheel indicators.

Like the one on the 10th, this operation was somehow overlooked when the Form 541 was written up. Buckley's hand-written Operational Report simply says 'Again a very useful training exercise'.

Interestingly, the Form 540 and Form 541 pages for March are headed 'No. 75 (NZ) Squadron, Feltwell', a name and status that wasn't known until the following month; this suggests somebody typed up the forms several weeks after the event. Perhaps they simply overlooked the two operations.

The Breckon crew that flew on the squadron's second wartime operation on 13 March 1940.
Left to right: F/L Aubrey Breckon, F/O 'Popeye' Lucas, Sgt Robert Hughes, AC Thomas Mumby, AC Eric Albert and LAC Ted Williams. Taken while training at Feltwell. ('Popeye' Lucas collection, courtesy of the Lucas family)

~ ~ ~ ~ ~ ~ ~ ~

Notes & References

1. No. 75 (NZ) Squadron Operations Record Book, R.A.F. Form 541, March 1940, Ref: AIR/27/645/3, The National Archives (UK).

2. Operational Report for Operational Flight No. 1, 10 March 1940, Special Sweep over area of North Sea, M.W. Buckley collection.

3. F.J. Lucas Pilot's Log Book, 'Popeye' Lucas collection, courtesy of the Lucas family.

Seal of Approval

The excitement of operations was interrupted on 20 March when RAF Feltwell hosted a visit by a group of special VIPs and a day of pomp and ceremony, recognising the achievements of several airmen and the battle readiness of the unit.

The New Zealand High Commissioner, Mr Bill Jordan, had planned to visit both 'the New Zealand Unit' at Feltwell and No. 99 Squadron at Newmarket on the same day, to meet Maurice Buckley and his men, to meet other New Zealanders serving in No. 3 Group and to present the Distinguished Flying Medal (DFM) to Corporal CBG Knight RNZAF of 99 Squadron.[1]

Jordan was to drive up from London with the New Zealand Liaison Officer, Squadron Leader Sid Wallingford, his Assistant Liaison Officer, Squadron Leader Fred Newell, and Mr SR Skinner, Chief Clerk at New Zealand House. To save time, it was decided instead to hold a single event at Feltwell and have the New Zealanders from Newmarket and Mildenhall travel across to attend.

A Service photographer was arranged to record the occasion and to potentially provide a censored photo for the newspapers back in New Zealand. Other VIPs attending included the head of Bomber Command, Air Chief Marshal Sir Edgar Ludlow-Hewitt, who would present decorations to other airmen from 3 Group, and the Air Officer Commanding 3 Group, Air Vice-Marshal Jack Baldwin.

The march past of station personnel was led by the RAF Feltwell band, with Buckley leading the parade and Kay leading the foundation members of the New Zealand Squadron, followed by the rest of the squadron and a detachment of members of the Women's Auxiliary Air Force.

Baldwin, Jordan and station commander Group Captain Charles Modin were on the dais as Ludlow-Hewitt took the salute, followed by an inspection and presentation of decorations, including six DFMs.

The newspapers in New Zealand reported:[2]

> In company with Air Chief-Marshal Sir Edgar Ludlow-Hewitt, the High Commissioner for New Zealand, Mr W. J. Jordan inspected a large number of airmen in a hangar at an East Anglian bomber station, including New Zealand officers and men who recently carried out their first operation – a sweep over the North Sea.

At Sir Edgar's request, Mr Jordan presented the DFM recently awarded to Corporal C. B. G. Knight whose coolness and courage in maintaining wireless communication under intense enemy fire contributed to the success of the operation over Schilling Roads and Friesian Islands on December 14.

Twenty-seven-year-old Corporal Colin 'Tod' Knight, from Tolaga Bay, New Zealand, was one of the six Wigram-trained wireless specialists who sailed to England on the liner MS *Rangitane* in December 1938 to train on Wellingtons. While the other four were posted to Marham to join the 1st Mobile Flight, he and Corporal Jack Langridge had been nominated to stay on in England to help train the next batch of New Zealand airmen due to arrive to take part in the second ferry flight. According to the plan, they were expected to leave England in December to fly back to New Zealand.

Knight had still been with 99 Squadron at Mildenhall when war broke out and on 18 December 1939 was flying as wireless operator in Squadron Leader Andrew 'Square' McKee's crew, earning his DFM in the Schillig Roads action. Colin Knight was the first member of the Royal New Zealand Air Force (RNZAF) to be decorated in the Second World War. A New Zealander in the RAF, McKee was also at Feltwell that day, having been awarded the Distinguished Flying Cross for his part in the same action.

New Zealand High Commissioner Jordan greeted on arrival by ACM Ludlow-Hewitt and AVM Baldwin, while Sid Wallingford stands at attention in the background. RAF Feltwell, 20 March 1940. (M.W. Buckley collection) Below, Ludlow-Hewitt (left) and Baldwin. Taken by Royal Air Force photographer, F/L Bertrand John Henry Daventry. (IWM)

The RAF Feltwell band, followed by G/C Modin, the station commander. Wing Commander Buckley leads the New Zealand Squadron.
Below: G/C Modin, High Commissioner Jordan and ACM Ludlow-Hewitt taking the salute. (Both M.W. Buckley collection)

NZ Squadron airmen march past the saluting dais (M.W. Buckley collection)

Left to right: S/L Newell, W/C Buckley, Mr Jordan, G/C Modin, Mr Skinner and S/L Wallingford.
Taken in front of Wellington P9210. Below, inspecting the assembled airmen with W/C Buckley, Mr Jordan shakes hands with wireless specialist LAC Joe White, with LAC Donald McGlashan next and Sgt Thomas Read closest to the camera. Cpl Bill Steven is on the other side of Joe White. (Both Auckland War Memorial Museum)

High Commissioner Bill Jordan presents the DFM to Cpl Colin Knight. (Auckland War Memorial Museum)

The title page in the album of photos later presented to Mr Jordan[3] incorrectly describes Knight as a member of the New Zealand Squadron; at that point he was still with 99 Squadron. He was soon afterwards posted to Lossiemouth as an instructor with No. 20 Operational Training Unit where he badly injured his back in an Anson crash on 27 July.

Cpl Colin Beresford Graham Knight RNZAF. (Auckland War Memorial Museum)

In September 1940, he was posted to Feltwell to take up the role of No. 75 (New Zealand) Squadron's signals leader, a position he held until April 1941.

Sadly, his mate Jack Langridge never made it to the squadron. Jack was also still with 99 Squadron when war broke out, taking part in the first raid of the war, targeting Kiel Canal, on 4 September. Later, on leave, he had been involved in a car accident which killed his friend, and then, while convalescing, the rest of his crew were lost on operations.

In February 1940, Jack was posted to No. 149 Squadron, Mildenhall where he served under Squadron Leader Wilfred Collett RNZAF, who was also from Gisborne. On 12 April 1940 Jack was flying as a wireless operator in a formation of 6 Wellingtons led by Collett near Stavanger, Norway, when they were attacked by German fighters. His Wellington is presumed to have been shot down into the sea and all but one of the crew were lost without trace. Corporal Jack Harry Langridge was the first member of the RNZAF to be killed in action in the war, only 21 years old, and is remembered on Panel 28 of the Runnymede Memorial.[2]

After the presentations, the VIPs were given lunch, with Jordan staying on for a tour of the station.

According to *The Otago Daily Times*:[3]

> After lunch Mr Jordan was conducted round the station by Group Captain Modin. He saw the mess rooms, the hospital, the administrative control rooms, the crew quarters, and a Link trainer, which was demonstrated for him.

He climbed into a Wellington bomber and the chief points of interest were explained to him.

Afterwards Flying Officers J. N. Collins and J. Adams (both of Christchurch), W. H, Coleman (Devonport), and N. Williams (New Plymouth) took off in a Wellington for a demonstration flight.

Mr Jordan (with W/C Buckley) meets F/O Neville Williams and his crew, just prior to boarding a Wellington and observing operation of the gun turrets. Williams far end, next is P/O Richard Hogg (2nd pilot), then Sgt Donald Mackay, AC Harold Smith, AC William Nevill and AC Lewis White. This crew had flown a Special Sweep the day before (19 March 1940). (Auckland War Memorial Museum[4])

~ ~ ~ ~ ~ ~ ~ ~

Notes & References

1. 'Visit of the High Commissioner for New Zealand to Units of No.3 (Bomber) Group' (SECRET), memo from NZLO Sidney Wallingford, 13 March 1940, M.W. Buckley collection.

2. Wellington P9266 OJ-F of 149 Squadron was shot down and crashed into the sea; Langridge's body was not recovered. The Runnymede Memorial near Egham, Surrey, is dedicated to members of the air force lost in the Second World War with no known grave. The names of 20,456 men and women from air forces of the British Empire are engraved into the stone walls.

3. 'Just Doing My Job', *The Otago Daily Times*, 29 April 1940.

4. Photo album 'Presented to W.J. Jordan Esq., High Commissioner for New Zealand, on the occasion of his visit to RAF STATION FELTWELL, to confer, on behalf of His Majesty, the Distinguished Flying Medal upon Corporal CBG Knight, NEW ZEALAND SQUADRON', 20 March 1940, Auckland War Memorial Museum.

Mr Jordan meeting members of F/O John Collins's crew; shaking hands with Eric Albert, Stan Brooks with goggles on head. Mr Skinner and W/C Buckley at left. (IWM, C1025)

First Blood

Parades and presentations over, it was back to work the next day with crews carrying out air-firing practice over The Wash and formation flying.

On 25 March, things got even more serious when three crews were briefed for a nighttime reconnaissance and *Nickel* (leaflet dropping) raid over Germany. It would be the unit's first operation over enemy territory.

Fred 'Popeye' Lucas recalled, since all were so keen to go, the pilots tossed for the job. The lucky winners were Cyril Kay (with Trevor Freeman as 2nd pilot), John Collins (with Don Harkness) and John Adams (with Geordie Larney). They took P9206, P9207 and P9212 up on night-flying tests in the late afternoon and were due to take off at 8:00pm, but the operation was eventually cancelled due to the weather. After a nervous wait, the crews were stood down at 10:05pm.

On the 27th, the same three crews went through a similar briefing and preparation, but this time the weather was deemed 'satisfactory'. They were detailed to drop their leaflets over three separate areas inside Germany: Brunswick, Ulzen and Luneburg.

> **27/03/1940 – Operational.**
> **Three Aircraft carried out reconnaissance and Nickel operations over the following areas, as detailed in No.3 Group Form B 102 dated 26.3.40**
>
> Wellington IA P9206 'A' – Brunswick area
>
> S/L Cyril Eyton 'Cyrus' Kay OBE RNZAF – Captain & Pilot
> P/O Trevor Owen Freeman RNZAF NZ1026 – 2nd Pilot
> Sgt Jim Whitlaw Carter RAFVR 527740 – Navigator
> LAC Ronald Alexander John Anderson RNZAF – Wireless Operator[1]
> AC Gilbert Ernest Adams RAF 632805 – Front Gunner
> P/O Alfred Basil Charles RAFVR 76005 – Rear Gunner
>
> Take Off: 10:30 – Landed: 7:20
> Flight Time: 08:50
>
> Wellington IA P9207 'C' – Ulzen area
>
> F/O John Noel Collins RNZAF NZ2513 – Captain & Pilot
> P/O Donald Joseph Harkness RAF 41694 – 2nd Pilot
> Sgt George Thorpe RAFVR 523426 – Navigator
> AC Francis William Green RAFVR 581283 – Wireless Operator
> AC John Stanley 'Stan' Brooks RAFVR 622115 – Front Gunner
> AC John Webster Gibb, RAF 632040 – Rear Gunner
>
> Take Off: 10:40 – Landed: 8:15
> Flight Time: 09:35
>
> Wellington IA P9212 'F' – Luneberg area
>
> F/O John 'Jack' Adams RNZAF NZ1027 – Captain & Pilot
> P/O Geordie Keith Larney RAF 33582 – 2nd Pilot

Sgt William Alfred Allinson RAF 526281 – Navigator
AC Herbert James Hawkins 'Bert' Kitson RAF 625948 – Wireless Operator
AC Douglas Reginald 'Reg' Day RAFVR 632887 – Front Gunner
AC Jack Gibbs RAFVR 625697– Rear Gunner

Take Off: 10:50 – Landed: 8:20
Flight Time: 09:30

Squadron Leader Kay remembered:

> It was to be a simple enough operation – merely the dropping of propaganda leaflets in selected towns in North Germany, but for us, the participants, it was the testing time. This flight would show whether our training had been sound and of a comparable standard to that of the experienced R.A.F. squadrons, so it was not without interest in Command Headquarters when we at last climbed aboard, waved a cheery good-bye to our envious companions, and roared heavily down the sluggish runway.[2]

Kay, Collins and Adams took off at ten-minute intervals between 10:30 and 10:50pm and made their way independently to their targets using dead reckoning and, in Kay's case, astro navigation. The briefing had described the weather as 'satisfactory' but Kay described it as 'miserable':

> The light was already fading from the leaden sky as we set course over the North Sea, and it was perhaps with a feeling of satisfaction that I gave permission for the gunners to test their weapons. As the front gun spat out its response in a vicious spurt of flame the aircraft shuddered and the light reflected eerily back, to be followed by the acrid tang of the burnt cordite wafting pungently past the cockpit.
>
> The rear gunner reported over the intercom, 'Guns in order, skipper,' and only then did I feel we were really at war.

Their path took them up the middle of the North Sea at 10,000 feet, to avoid neutral Holland and Belgium, then a right turn just short of Heligoland to head down into Germany, crossing the coast at Dorum, near Hamburg.

As if the danger of flying in the dark over heavily defended Germany wasn't enough, Kay's aircraft was hit by lightning and the wireless transmitter burnt out. The heating system also stopped working and the astrodome froze over, the temperature in the aircraft dropping to -28° Celsius! It would later be described as the worst flying night in four years.

All three targets were found and the leaflets were dropped from heights between 7,000 and 10,000 feet over the towns of Brunswick, Ulzen and Luneburg, and from 14,000 feet over Hooge. Some flak was experienced over Hamburg and the German Frisian Islands, with searchlight activity near Hamburg and the islands of Nordeoney, Wantroog and Sylt. Only one enemy aircraft was seen, in the vicinity of Amrum, but it immediately switched off its navigation lights and disappeared.

With heavy cloud building, stronger winds than forecast and driving rain on the return trip, their problems weren't over, as Adams and his crew discovered when, on their ETA, they found themselves not over Feltwell but over a large, fully lit city! It was Amsterdam and Adams decided it would be safest to fly south across the city and land in France. His front gunner, 'Reg' Day recalled:[3]

> The air force at Amsterdam had other ideas and sent up two fighters to chase us out over the North Sea. So down to sea-level came John with the Wimpy, heading for Feltwell. Unfortunately, violent electrical storms forced us south, so John informed me and Jack Gibbs, the rear gunner, to tidy up in case we had to land on the sea and be prepared to release the dinghy.

> The engines were now getting red hot through lack of oil so Jack and I had to use the emergency oil pump. We were still in trouble and just about ready to pancake when John came over the intercom to say he could see the White Cliffs of Dover.
>
> Once over land, he shot up every aerodrome from Dover to Feltwell and we were last back after a 9½-hour flight, and almost drained of fuel.

Not so lucky was a No. 77 Squadron Whitley, also out 'nickeling' that night and straying into Dutch airspace. It was shot down in flames near Rotterdam by a Fokker G.IA of the Dutch Air Force, with one crew member killed and four interned.

Several accounts of those early days nominate this raid as the squadron's first war operation. In his own memoir, *The Restless Sky*, Kay states the night of 27/28 March was the first, as does BG Clare in *Early Operations in Bomber Command* (NZ Govt. official) and HL Thompson in *New Zealanders in the Air War*. The four 'Special Sweeps', though officially operations and carried out in wartime and in contested airspace, appear to have been thought of more as training exercises. The fifth effort was certainly more dramatic and dangerous than those, and for the first time took the squadron into Germany, so was seen as a worthy 'first' to write into the history books.

As Maurice Buckley later wrote:

> Still, it was a beginning, and how glad we all were when those machines came back from their raid. I think every man of the squadron, ground crews and maintenance included, were there to welcome them back when they landed.[4]

It would the first of many times that he would welcome Kay back, just like in Cundall's painting. Buckley's welcomes would become part of squadron folklore. 'Good show! Good show!' he would tell the men, no matter how successful or otherwise their trip had been.

Air Vice-Marshal Jack Baldwin wrote to Buckley on the 31st, congratulating him on the effort, impressed they had undertaken a nine-hour trip 'on what was really their first try-out'.[5]

Baldwin made his plans for the unit clear. He noted that, now it was operational, he was arranging for more aircraft to be allocated and offered New Zealander Wilfred Collett as a second flight commander: 'I am full out to build the flight up to a Squadron.'

In fact, the very next day, on 1 April, the Air Ministry issued instructions for No. 75 (N.Z.) Squadron to be formed 'round the existing New Zealand Flight at Feltwell'. No. 75 (New Zealand) Squadron RAF officially came into being three days later, on 4 April 1940.

The name of the new squadron brought with it a proud history going all the way back to the formation of 75 Squadron on 1 October 1916 at Goldington, Bedford, as a Home Defence unit of the Royal Flying Corps. Back then it was equipped with B.E.2.C, D and E aircraft. It was disbanded in June 1919 but then, as part of the RAF's expansion, in March 1937, it was reformed as a heavy bomber squadron, based at Driffield, Yorkshire, operating Vickers Virginias and Avro Ansons. By early 1940, it was flying out of Harwell as a Group Pool training unit for No. 3 Group, Bomber Command.

Unzensuriert!

Die Redensarten von „Diktatur der Demokratien" und „Bedrohung Deutschlands" sind nichts als gemeine Lügen, mit denen man Euch

auf's Schlachtfeld treibt.

Hat Eure zensurierte Presse es gewagt, Mr. Chamberlains Erklärung in Birmingham zu veröffentlichen? In dieser Rede sprach Chamberlain über

Kriegsziele

und sagte:

„England begehrt keine fremden Länder... Wir kämpfen um den militaristischen Geist zu zerstören und die Anhäufung von Rüstung zu beseitigen, die ganz Europa und nicht zuletzt

Deutschland verarmt.

Nur durch die Vernichtung jenes militaristischen Geistes und der Rüstungen kann Europa vor

Bankrott und Ruin

bewahrt werden!"

Könnt Ihr leugnen, daß Armut, Elend, Inflation und

Bolschewismus

die Folgen eines ausgedehnten Krieges sein werden?

309

Propaganda leaflet quoting Prime Minister Chamberlain's Birmingham speech of 24 February 1940. 'Only through the destruction of this militaristic spirit and armament can Europe be preserved from bankruptcy and ruin.' (M.W. Buckley collection)

The crew that carried out the long-distance reconnaissance flight to Narvik, Norway, on 12 April 1940. Left to right: LAC Edwin Williams, F/L Aubrey Breckon, Lt Cdr FO Howie, Sgt Robert Hughes, P/O Donald Harkness and AC Thomas Mumby. (ref. PR9157, Air Force Museum of NZ)

Buckley's ally, Air Chief Marshal Edgar Ludlow-Hewitt, the chief of Bomber Command, had recently overseen the establishment of the new operational training units (OTU) to replace the Group Pool units; this meant 75 Squadron was to be absorbed into No. 15 OTU on 4 April. On that date, the '75 Squadron RAF' nameplate was given to the new squadron, with the prized 'New Zealand' identifier added in brackets. It was the first New Zealand squadron in the RAF, and the first 'Commonwealth' squadron of the war. No. 75 (New Zealand) Squadron RAF was allocated the squadron code 'AA'. However, as Baldwin had pointed out, it had yet to form a second flight and another seven weeks would pass before it reached full squadron strength.

Meanwhile, three aircraft had taken part in a searchlight cooperation exercise on the night of 30 March and another Special Sweep was ordered on 4 April. However, the three aircraft that took off at 8:25am were recalled for bad weather and were back on the ground by 9:55.

On the 6th, Aubrey Breckon, the two Williams and 'Bill' Coleman carried out another nickeling and reconnaissance operation over Germany (Neinberg, Bremen and Verden), an eight-hour round trip. The weather was perfect and, according to Breckon's report, searchlights were numerous and very active, but very little anti-aircraft fire was experienced. The only problem was when the Coleman crew in P9210 had their wireless transmitter fail on the return trip and they had to land away from base at Bircham Newton.

There was some frustration among the airmen at being tasked with leaflet-dropping; in Lucas's words, 'dropping bits of paper and getting shot at for our pains'. British government policy at this early stage of the war was to avoid any attack that might harm civilians, so bombing was restricted to isolated targets such as ships at sea, military transport and military aerodromes. Years later, 'Breck' Breckon would tell a story of bricks mysteriously disappearing from a Feltwell hangar repair project, taken by aircrew needing something more satisfying to drop on Hitler.[6] The budding squadron's next operation, however, was epic in nature and made both the newspapers and the record books.

Germany struck twice on 9 April, occupying Denmark and invading Norway by sea. A key goal was to seize the ice-free Norwegian port of Narvik and secure Germany's supply of Swedish iron ore, critical to the production of steel. In an attempt to stop the invasion, the Royal Navy had attacked German ships on the 10th, in the first naval Battle of Narvik, and now wanted to sail up the 50-mile-long Narvik fjord on the 13th to finish the job.

Flight Lieutenant Breckon and crew, along with another crew from No. 38 Squadron, were selected to carry out 'special duties' for the Navy. Attached to Coastal Command and flying out of RAF Wick in Scotland, they would fly a series of long-distance reconnaissance flights to Norway. Breckon's crew for the attachment was Pilot Officer Donald Harkness (2nd pilot), Sergeant Robert Hughes (observer), Leading Aircraftman Edwin 'Ted' Williams (wireless operator) and Aircraftman Thomas Mumby (gunner observer).

On the afternoon of 10 April, they flew to Bassingbourn to collect a Wellington Mark I (L4387) from No. 11 OTU. The aircraft was ex-operational, still carrying its old No. 215 Squadron code letters, 'LG-L', and had been fitted with long-range fuel tanks. However, wireless operator Ted Williams found it had no direction-finding loop so he had to find and fit one. The 38 Squadron crew, skippered by Pilot Officer George Crosby, was also there collecting a Wellington, L4339. They worked on their aircraft that night and, early the next morning, both Wellingtons left for Wick, Breckon calling in briefly to Feltwell on the way to pick up maintenance crew.

On arrival at Wick, around midday on the 11th, the commanding officer explained they were to be attached to No. 269 (General Reconnaissance) Squadron. They spent the rest of the afternoon checking and readying their aircraft for the trips. That night, Breckon's crew was told they had been chosen to make the first long-distance flight the following day.

At an early morning briefing, they were tasked with flying to Narvik to find out whether there were any enemy ships which might ambush British forces from the many inlets running off the main fjord. They were to take a Royal Navy observer (Lieutenant Commander FO Howie) with them for ship recognition and reporting.

Breckon and his crew took off into a squally north-west wind and worsening weather at 8:00am on the 12th, heading for a target 1,000 miles over the North Sea, and past the Arctic Circle. They made landfall five hours later and had some trouble finding the right fjord in the atrocious conditions. Ted Williams described the flight up the fjord in his operational report and in a later newspaper account:

> The weather was so bad that we could not fly higher than a thousand feet above sea-level. The further up we went the lower became the ceiling. The fjord began to narrow until huge rocks towered up on either side of us. Their peaks were hidden in dirty mist and sleet. Snow drifted down, so that soon we could only see a few yards ahead. The 'wind-locks' were terrific, bouncing and throwing us about until we had barely enough room to turn round.

Although they reached Narvik, flying at only 200 feet among low cloud and snowstorms, they had to turn back. Williams continued:

> Visibility was almost nil. Up till that moment we had been able to see the surface of the fjord. Now we could do so no longer. We went about and picked our way down the fjord again, feeling our way along the cliffs like a boat hugging the shore. Suddenly we saw once more the open sea.
>
> On the way back we saw a Junkers 86 bomber, evidently on the same kind of duty as we were. We circled round each other for a while and then both came to the conclusion it would be a good idea to make off for home.[7]

They had to endure a six-hour flight back over the North Sea, still in bad weather and only reaching Scotland as darkness fell. At 10:30 in the evening, after a flight of well over 2,000 miles, the Wellington finally touched down at Wick with only 37 gallons of petrol left in its tanks. With no automatic pilot fitted, Breckon and Harkness had manually flown the aircraft for 14 hours 30 minutes. It was one of the longest flights undertaken by a Wellington bomber and an RAF endurance record at the time.

The operation had been a success: they were able to report that Narvik Fjord was clear of enemy shipping up to within ten miles of the town. On the next day, the second Battle of Narvik was fought and eight German destroyers and one submarine were destroyed.

Unfortunately, the other crew were not so lucky.

On the afternoon of the 13th, Pilot Officer George Crosby and his 38 Squadron crew took off from Wick in borrowed Wellington L4339 to carry out a reconnaissance of Værnes airport at Trondheim. They successfully navigated the North Sea and found the target but, while in the vicinity, their aircraft was damaged by a German fighter. They managed to make it most of the way back across the North Sea but, at 12:04am, a Mayday message was sent; not long afterwards, the Wellington is thought to have crashed into the sea about 22 miles north-east of Whitby, North Yorkshire, killing all five crew members and their Royal Navy observer.

Back at Feltwell, the squadron was on standby to find and attack the German fleet, in particular the battlecruisers *Scharnhorst* and *Gneisenau*. On the 12th, Kay, Collins, 'Bill' Williams and Adams joined eight Wellingtons from No. 37 Squadron to search for a German destroyer but were driven down to almost sea level by the terrible conditions off the Norwegian coast and had to split up and make their own way home. 'With the exception of three twin-ruddered aircraft, believed to be M.E. 110's [*sic*], seen going away in the distance, no enemy aircraft or surface vessels were located.' What they were going to do if they found the ship is not known, as there is no record of bombs being carried. After passing through a heavy rain squall, Adams managed to spot Kay's Wellington, P9206 AA-A, and they flew back in formation.

Despite the weather, raids across the North Sea were now becoming regular. Collins and Neville Williams had the privilege of dropping the squadron's first bombs in anger when they successfully attacked Stavanger aerodrome in Norway on the 17th, dropping a stick of bombs each on the runway from 5,000 feet despite the attentions of the local searchlight and light flak defences. Conditions were again inhospitable and the heating in Collins's aircraft failed; after four hours in the rear turret, Stan Brooks was covered in frost and icicles, and his thermos flask of hot chocolate had frozen solid.

Adams had taken off with them but, about an hour into the trip, Bert Kitson, the wireless operator, reported smoke coming from behind the fuse panel so they turned for home. By removing the fuses, Kitson was able to fix the problem and they got back safely – 'No trouble was experienced in landing with a full bomb load.' The other three crews all returned unscathed from what was a seven-hour round trip.

Then, on 21 April, Adams, Coleman and Bill Williams took off at 6:30pm for a night attack on Aarlborg aerodrome in Denmark. They encountered strong searchlight activity and intense flak, and four enemy aircraft over the aerodrome, which fortunately did not attack. Coleman reported 'slight grazes' to his

Stavanger aerodrome (left of centre, partially obscured by cloud), 17 April 1940. (AAN Breckon collection, Air Force Museum of NZ)

Wellington, P9212, but the trip was otherwise uneventful and the crews made it safely back to Feltwell between 1:05 and 1:50 in the morning.

On the 22nd, Breckon and his crew made another reconnaissance flight from Wick across to Norway, to Trondheim, the target that had proved fatal for Crosby's crew. They took off much earlier this time, 2:00am, and in much better weather, arriving over Kristiansund at 4:30, tasked with photographing and observing Trondheim, the frozen lake adjoining, and the aerodrome at Værnes, thought to have been occupied by the Germans. The snow-covered landscape allowed excellent photographs to be taken of the mountains, fjords, ships, the township and its aerodrome.

Ted Williams described the trip:

> Everything was under snow and peaceful and quiet as we flew up the fiord. We zig-zagged over and about Trondheim and took 72 photographs. On a frozen lake there were 22 aircraft snowed under and abandoned. There were 16 seaplanes in the harbour and four troopships. The Germans had apparently landed.
>
> After we'd got our photographs, we flew on to an aerodrome which had been abandoned owing to the snow. When we came back over the town we ran into a heavy barrage of A.A. fire, for the Jerries had woken up by this time. We were at about 3,000 feet and we caught a packet in the front screen. After a bit of dodging and diving, we managed to get out of it.
>
> Then we passed over two German warships, and they let us have it too. It didn't worry us a lot, and by the time we got to the entrance to the fiord I had managed to send over the air all the information we had collected.[7]

Breckon was slightly injured in one eye when the flak smashed his windscreen but fortunately had his flying goggles on his head and was able to pull them down for protection from the vicious draught. Still, the four-hour trip home must have been bitterly cold and uncomfortable.

Among the set of beautiful aerial photos taken by the crew that day is a startling vertical view of 22 *Luftwaffe* aircraft that had been forced to land on the frozen lake, Jonsvatnet, after finding nearby Værnes snowed in. Acting on the information Williams radioed back, carrier-based aircraft of the Fleet Air Arm bombed the lake later that day 'to good effect'.[8]

The build-up to full squadron strength continued during April with another five pilots arriving – two English RAF pilot officers on the 6th (Richard Curtis and Frank De Labouchere-Sparling), and three Wigram-trained RNZAF pilot officers on the 17th (Eric Best, Arthur Humphreys and Charles Pownall).

Buckley's air gunner stocks were also boosted with RAF pilot officers posted in: Leonard Hockey (to take up the role of gunnery officer) on the 6th; then John Ferris, George Fletcher, Walter Horley, Geoffrey Horsfall, William Rayner and Sedgewick Webster on the 22nd. On 24 April, 20 RNZAF air gunners arrived at Feltwell.

The group had trained in New Zealand at Ohakea on Vildebeests and sailed from Auckland on the liner RMS *Remuera* on 20 February. All held the rank of leading aircraftman and needed to complete advanced gunnery training in England before they could get their full air gunner's ticket and sergeant's stripes.

Ground training was carried out at Feltwell, but the squadron couldn't spare operational aircraft so the men were sent away for air training to other squadrons and OTUs. They returned to Feltwell fully qualified about a month later, four of them subsequently posted out to No. 149 Squadron; the rest stayed on at Feltwell.

The aerial photo of 22 *Luftwaffe* aircraft on the frozen Jonsvatnet, near Trondheim, Norway, 22 May 1940. (AAN Breckon collection, Air Force Museum of NZ)

More and better aircraft were arriving, the squadron receiving its first two brand-new Mark ICs (R3157 and R3158) on the 19th and a third (R3159) the following day. More would arrive in May. On 3 May, one of the two remaining Wellington Mark Is, L4340 (NZ302, which apart from a short 15-min hop across to Methwold on 21.4.40 had not been in the air since arriving at Feltwell) was flown out for good to No. 22 Maintenance Unit, Silloth.

L4355 (NZ304), however, had been kept active for training purposes, recoded 'Z', and flying air tests and local and cross-country sorties in April and May. The last of the five original Wellingtons, it was finally transferred out to No. 11 OTU at Bassingbourn on 17 June.

Operations were aborted on the 1st and 3rd of May, but cross country, air firing, high- and low-level bombing and formation flying training continued.

On 7 May, another attempt was made to bomb Stavanger aerodrome but despite having successfully made their way across the North Sea, and the excitement of seeing a submarine of unknown nationality, Collins (who was leading the formation, promoted to Flight Lieutenant three days previously), Coleman and Neville Williams were thwarted by heavy cloud over Norway. An attempt to get above the cloud resulted in icing at 11,000 feet, forcing them to descend and jettison their loads in the sea on the way home.

Everything changed on 10 May when Germany invaded France and the neutral countries of the Netherlands and Belgium. New Prime Minister Winston Churchill immediately gave approval for the RAF's long-delayed plan to attack German industrial centres. It was the end of the 'Phoney War'. Collins and Neville and Bill Williams were immediately given the opportunity to take the fight to the new front.

Waalhaven military base and aerodrome at Rotterdam had fallen to the Germans on the morning of the 10th and, along with 33 other 3 Group Wellingtons, the three Feltwell crews were detailed to carry out individual attacks that night. Each Wellington carried twelve 250-lb general-purpose (GP) bombs, dropping their loads from only 2,000 feet and doing as much damage as they could to the airfield – 'All turrets used their guns on buildings.' The defences were not strong and no enemy aircraft were seen, although Collins noted 'many fires seen in and around Rotterdam'. 'All aircraft were safely landed at Base by 02.50 hours on 11th May 1940.'

Together with counter-attacks by Dutch ground forces and a separate attack by RAF Blenheims, the 3 Group bombing caused casualties, significant losses of *Luftwaffe* aircraft, damage to the airfield and temporary disruption to the German airlift, but the Germans eventually held.

That day, four more New Zealand pilots were posted in: Pilot Officers Edward Cameron, Douglas Gilmour, Malcolm Macfarlane and Duncan McArthur (all RAF but RNZAF Wigram-trained). Air gunner Pilot Officer Malcolm Miller was posted in on the 15th.

May 12 was a red-letter day – the new bomber squadron finally got to bomb Germany itself. Taking off at 9:10pm, Kay, Breckon and Coleman carried out individual attacks on Krefeld aerodrome, bombing from 10–11,000 feet in the face of intense searchlight activity. Each Wellington carried twelve 250-lb GP bombs, half of which were fused with delay timers of 3, 6, 8 and 12 hours. Leftover bombs were dropped on two transport columns and the three crews reported seeing numerous fires and plenty of anti-aircraft and searchlight activity in the Rhine area and over the Netherlands, but only one enemy aircraft near Antwerp. They were all safely back on the ground at Feltwell by 2:00am.

Further attacks on targets in Germany, Belgium and occupied France were made on the 15th, 16th, 17th and 19th with varying degrees of success, and worrying reports of 'friendly' fire on the way out from over-enthusiastic anti-aircraft batteries around Felixstowe. By now the main priority was to assist the British Expeditionary Force, which had been driven back across France, and individual hit-and-run attacks known as 'rhubarbs' became the norm, striking bridges, road junctions, convoys and mechanised troop concentrations. Crews were also instructed to immediately report any significant enemy road or rail movements. Because of the fast-moving battlefront, they were issued with what were known as 'BOMLIN' co-ordinates before each raid to help avoid bombing their own forces.

Things were not going well on the ground; returning home on the night of the 19th/20th, Breckon reported seeing Dunkirk burning fiercely. The raid into Belgium that night also resulted in the squadron's first battle injury.

Trevor Freeman's aircraft was approaching woods at Givet from only 500 feet, intending to drop incendiaries, when it was hit by machine-gun fire from the ground. The aircraft was damaged, disabling the bomb-release mechanism. Pilot Officer Charles Pownall, the 2nd pilot, caught a bullet in his right shoulder. He would be out of action for two months. John Collins reported stiff flak opposition:

> Aircraft was hit twice. Once in the tailplane and the other passed from the Starboard side of the rear turret through the Port side missing my rear gunner's bottom.

Worse was to come.

A record eight aircraft were put up by the squadron on the night of the 21st for individual attacks on pontoons and bridges around Aachen and Dinant in Belgium to try to slow the progress of the German Army. Squadron Leader Collett was flying his first operation with the squadron.

Flight Lieutenant John Collins and his crew in Wellington R3157, coded AA-H, were on their way to bomb the bridge at Dinant when, just east of Tournai, heavy flak ripped into the starboard engine, starting a fire that threatened to spread to the fuselage.

> Wireless operator Brooks, now doubling as front gunner, tried to extinguish the flames with the fire extinguisher, but made no impression. At the same time, Collins turned to port, trying to put the fire out and hoping to make a forced landing over friendly territory, but the fire became unquenchable and he gave the order to bail out.
>
> Over the intercom he told his second pilot, P/O Frank De Labouchere-Sparling and navigator Sgt/Observer George Thorpe to open the bulk-head door as they bailed out through the hatch as did rear gunner P/O Hockey, who as gunnery officer, had just arrived at Feltwell. He had volunteered to go that night 'just to see what it was like'.
>
> Stan Brooks made his way into the inferno in the fuselage stepping over the open hatch and found his parachute on the bed under the astro hatch surrounded by flames but apparently still useable. The interior was now a blazing mass, with all the fabric burnt away. F/L Collins was wrestling the controls, his parachute lying in the rack alongside the bomb aimer's position. Brooks grabbed it, trying to hook it onto his pilot's chest hooks, but could only reach one hook, and Collins was yelling at him, 'Get out, get out quick' - and Brooks glancing at the altimeter saw he had only a few hundred feet in which to parachute to safety. He dived out of the hatch headfirst as the Wellington began to roll and just then the bomb load exploded ... [9]

John 'Stan' Brooks was blown upwards by the blast, suspended momentarily amongst his parachute canopy. The explosion may well have saved his life as he had jumped at such a low altitude. He landed hard, but thankfully in one piece, in a ploughed field near Kain, right in the middle of a battle zone. Hiding his parachute under a hedgerow, he started crawling along it towards an old stone mill when he was suddenly caught in the full glare of a field searchlight! The next day he was taken to a farmhouse for interrogation by the *Luftwaffe* and there he was reunited with Thorpe and Hockey. The three became the squadron's first prisoners of war (POW).

Tragically, De Labouchere-Sparling was killed, possibly the victim of ground fire as he parachuted down. He is buried at Kain Communal Cemetery near Tournai. John Collins was also killed, although he appears to have been blown clear of the aircraft when it exploded.[10] His body fell well away from the wreckage, landing with parachute intact and no signs of burns in a swampy area on the opposite (south) side of the river Scheldt.

In the chaos of the ground fighting, it was about three weeks before his body was recovered and, sadly, either his identity could not be confirmed or it was not recorded.

Flight Lieutenant John Noel Collins was the first RNZAF pilot to be killed in the war. To this day he lies in a grave at Froyennes marked 'An Airman of the 1939–45 War – RAF – 21st May 1940. A Man Known only to God'. Only one aircraft was shot down in the area that night so the 'unknown' airman can only be Collins, but efforts over the years to have the Commonwealth War Graves Commission add his name to the headstone have so far been unsuccessful.

F/L John Noel Collins and P/O Francis Albert Gabriel Fernand Joseph De Labouchere-Sparling.
(Anna Rhodes-Sayer, Heidi Domeisen)

Buckley later referred to that night in a radio broadcast back to New Zealand:

> Then came the time when the first machine did not return. How we waited for it and for days hoped against hope that they were safely down somewhere in England. The feeling of loss over a machine not returning never seems to grow less but the memory of that first one remains particularly poignant.[11]

It was weeks before news came through that three of the crew had survived as POWs; it was not until after the war that details emerged of what had happened that night. The significance of the squadron's first operational loss was acknowledged by Air Chief Marshal Charles Portal, the new Commander-In-Chief of Bomber Command[12], in a letter to Buckley on the 24th: 'It must have been a great blow to you when Collins and his crew failed to return on Tuesday night.'[13]

It certainly was a great blow; the first loss, the loss of one of the 12 foundation pilots, the loss of five good men and their aircraft.

And the first of many difficult letters Buckley, as commanding officer, would have to write to the families of the missing.

~ ~ ~ ~ ~ ~ ~ ~

Notes & References

1. The Form 541 disagrees with the Operational Report, listing LAC Edwin Peter 'Ted' Williams RNZAF NZ38235 as wireless operator. Anderson flew with Kay on the previous and subsequent operations, so seems the more likely of the two options.

2. AVM Cyril Kay, CB CBE DFC, *The Restless Sky*, George G. Harrap, 1964.

3. Norman Franks, *Forever Strong: The Story of 75 Squadron RNZAF, 1916–1990*, Random Century, 1991.

4. Suggested script for Group Captain Buckley's Broadcast to New Zealand, letter to H.L. Saunders, Air Ministry, 20th of August 1941, M.W. Buckley collection.

5. Letter from M Baldwin, HQ 3 Group, to W/C Buckley, Feltwell, 31 March 1940, M.W. Buckley collection.

6. 'The Bold Have Wings', radio documentary 1958, Ngā Taonga Sound & Vision.

7. 'Veterans of the Skies', *Evening Post*, 12 November 1940.

8. Kenneth R. Hancock, *New Zealand at War*, A.H. & A.W. Reed, 1946.

9. Lorie Lucas, *Popeye's War*, self-published, 1996.

10. Heidi Domeisen, relative of Frank De Labouchere-Sparling, personal communications with author.

11. Suggested script for Group Captain Buckley's Broadcast to New Zealand.

12. ACM Sir Edgar Ludlow-Hewitt was replaced as Commander-In-Chief of Bomber Command by ACM Charles Portal in April 1940. Progress in the rearmament and expansion of the bomber force was perceived as too slow, with Ludlow-Hewitt's withdrawal of some front-line squadrons to form his new operational training units a contributing factor. However, some viewed the change in leadership as more about politics than capability.

13. Letter from AM Portal, HQ Bomber Command to W/C Buckley, Feltwell, 24th May 1940, M.W. Buckley collection.

A New Fighting Force

Two Wellington Mark IAs of No. 75 (NZ) Squadron – P9206 AA-A nearest (S/L Cyrus Kay's regular aircraft), and L7784 AA-D – June 1940. (RNZAF official via Andy Thomas)

After the sad loss of the Collins crew, things at Feltwell took a happier turn on 23 May with the wedding of Flight Lieutenant Aubrey Breckon and Dana Waugh at the little station church, St. George's. It was a real squadron affair; Feltwell Chaplain Squadron Leader the Reverend Arthur Kayll officiated, Breckon's best man was Flying Officer Neville Williams and the bride was given away by Squadron Leader 'Cyrus' Kay. After the ceremony, a reception was held in the Feltwell officers mess, with photos showing Maurice Buckley and most of his pilots in attendance. Celebrations must have been reasonably restrained, however, with an operation scheduled for that night.

Six Wellingtons were detailed to attack various targets in Belgium but, just prior to take-off, Neville Williams's aircraft developed engine problems and he had to pull out. Squadron Leaders Kay and Wilfred Collett were both on the Battle Order, as were Flying Officers 'Jack' Adams, 'Bill' Coleman and 'Popeye' Lucas.

Adams led them off at 9:15pm to make separate attacks on a bridge, railway line and crossroads, all in the Yvoir and Profondeville region, south of Namur. Unable to locate his target, Coleman found and bombed a convoy of 50 vehicles on the road between Wavre and Gembloux, and dropped another stick of six bombs on a row of searchlights at Namur. Cloud and searchlights made their work more difficult, but no enemy aircraft were seen and all crews were safely back on the ground at Feltwell by 1:50 the next morning.

Operational reports in these early days[1] were quite formal ('I have the honour to submit ...,' etc.) and quite detailed, including petrol and oil consumption and mileages.

Bomb loads usually comprised 40-lb, 250-lb or 500-lb General Purpose (GP) bombs, and sometimes cases of small 4-lb incendiary bombs, in combinations made up to the Wimpy's maximum load of around 4,000 lbs. GP bombs could be dropped individually or in multiples at set intervals (a 'stick'). Bomb fuses could be set to NDT (No Delay Time) or DA (Delayed Action) to explode 3, 6, 8, 12 or even 18 hrs after being dropped.

Bombing techniques were still being developed and crews were working out the most effective ways of achieving accuracy while trying to negotiate the weather conditions, escape searchlights and avoid flak and ground fire. Their reports tell of attacks made from heights anywhere between 12,000 and 2,000 feet, with some pilots preferring to fly level and some utilising shallow dives before release. By April–May 1940, the high-speed, powered dive was generally becoming the preferred method. Cyrus Kay described one technique he used:

> Anticipating his call of 'Bombs away!', I threw the machine into a steep banking turn, both as a measure of evasion and in an endeavour to shower the 250-pound general-purpose bombs and the crates of incendiaries in as wide an arc as possible.

Night fighters were scarce and, if conditions were against them, the bombers could afford to loiter around the target for up to an hour, waiting for visibility to improve or an opportunity on the ground to present itself. However, there was a sense of futility in these relatively ineffective individual attacks. The attempt to save France was by now doomed and what was left of the British Expeditionary Force was gathering on the beach at Dunkirk, hoping for evacuation to England.

Eight Wellingtons were put up for operations on the 25th, two to carry out reconnaissance between Courtrai and Brussels and six to attack an enemy ammunition dump three miles west of Trelon. Adams and Breckon left first but, in poor weather, couldn't detect any troop movements in the assigned area so dropped their bomb loads on two railway junctions and a main road before heading home. The main group took off at 11:00pm, with Squadron Leader Kay the senior pilot, but, again, one aircraft developed engine problems as it headed out over the coast of England and had to turn back for home. Four crews found the target and started fires, suggesting a successful attack, but Kay saved some of his load to drop on a searchlight battery and a gun position. Two crews failed to identify the target due to rain, sleet and cloud cover, but dropped their bombs on surrounding woods and roads. Captains reported plenty of searchlight activity but only one enemy aircraft, which didn't attack. Despite heavy rain and icing, they were all home safely by 4:00 in the morning.

On the night of the 28th, seven No. 75 (NZ) Squadron Wellingtons took off between 11:00pm and 12:45am to make individual attacks on enemy troop positions, with Squadron Leader Collett leading the way. He, Trevor Freeman and Fred Lucas had been briefed to attack a target at Roeselare, near Dunkirk, while Breckon, Adams, Coleman and Neville Williams were to bomb a target at Menin, a few miles further to the west.

Visibility was terrible, with broken cloud extending from 1,000 to 12,000 feet, and intermittent thunder and rainstorms. As a result, only three crews were able to positively identify their aiming point. Freeman dive-bombed the Roeselare target twice from 2,500 feet, dropping a stick of six 250 pounders each time. He claimed direct hits and many lights extinguished. Lucas found the same target but was unable to bomb due to a switch that had inadvertently been set to 'Safe'! Neville Williams, with a load of six 500 pounders, found the Menin target but had to circle for 20 minutes trying to confirm his identification through the pall of smoke. Two parachute flares eventually enabled him to do so; he delivered a single bomb from 5,000 feet, before dropping to 3,500 feet to drop two more, finally running back over the target at 4,000 feet to let go the last three. Collett reported widespread fires around Lille, heavy artillery fire from both sides and oil tanks blazing furiously at Dunkirk.

They flew home to low cloud over East Anglia and, with fog at Feltwell, five of the Wellingtons had to divert to Mildenhall. All were back on the ground by 3:50am.

~ ~ ~ ~ ~ ~ ~ ~

An entry in the squadron Operations Record Book for 21 May 1940 records:

> Formation of new flight.
>
> Additional personnel posted to Unit for formation of extra flight, so making unit into a Squadron and no longer just a flight. Divided into two flights, 'A' and 'B'.[2]

Maurice Buckley was finally about to see his vision of a full-strength, fully operational New Zealand bomber squadron become a reality.

The squadron was proving itself daily as a fighting force, and a valuable contributor to the efforts of Bomber Command, and now the last pieces of the plan were falling into place to bring it to full squadron status. Squadron Leader Kay was already commanding 'A' Flight. As promised by Baldwin, Flight Lieutenant Wilfred Collett had been posted in from No. 149 Squadron on 5 May and promoted to acting squadron leader, ready to take up his appointment as flight commander. Pilot Officer William Mitchell RAF had been posted in as squadron adjutant on the 25th.

On the 29th, Collett was officially appointed flight commander of the newly established 'B' Flight and 75 (New Zealand) Squadron finally reached full strength.

Buckley wrote a memorandum to mark the milestone, titled 'Formation of No 75 (NZ) Squadron from the New Zealand Flight':

> Today, May 29th, 1940, No. 75(NZ) Squadron is officially increased from a Flight to a fully established Squadron, and I wish to place on record the merits of the original N.C.O.'s [sic] and airmen who formed the New Zealand Flight at Marham on 1st June 1939.[3]

It was typical of 'Buck' that he should give full credit to his ground staff, first mentioning his original righthand men, Roberts, Read and Steven, plus his four wireless specialists. He must have felt tremendous pride when he noted that, in the year since the unit was established:

> The standard of maintenance of these original members of the New Zealand Flight, and the exceptional ability of the pilots themselves, has enabled the Squadron to carry out all jobs without a forced landing or accident of any description.
>
> It is regretted that the original programme of flying thirty Wellington aeroplanes to New Zealand could not be proceeded with, as the assured success of this venture would, I am sure, have been ample reward to the original members of the New Zealand Flight as listed hereunder.

He then went on to list by name each of the 31 fitters, riggers, mechanics and technicians who had made up his team in those early days.

It had started off as a temporary, bare bones operation, located on the opposite side of the globe, operating and maintaining five large aircraft from borrowed office and hangar space, scrounging supplies and loaning staff. Now it was a fully professional unit in the Royal Air Force. It was a job well done but, at the same time, it was just the beginning.

Buckley would command the new squadron for the first six months of its life and then have the privilege of overseeing another six months from the station commander's office at Feltwell. But, for now, he would have felt great satisfaction in the knowledge the squadron could take a full part in the war as an effective and respected first-line fighting unit.

~~~~~~~~

Group Captain Maurice William Buckley MBE RNZAF, Feltwell, 1941. (Air Force Museum of NZ)

Notes & References

1. No. 75 Squadron Operations Record Book – Appendices, Ref: AIR/27/649, The National Archives (UK).

2. No. 75 (NZ) Squadron Operations Record Book, R.A.F. Form 540, May 1940, Ref: AIR/27/645/6, The National Archives (UK).

3. Formation of No 75 (NZ) Squadron from the New Zealand Flight, letter by W/C M.W. Buckley, 29 March 1940, M.W. Buckley collection.

Postscripts

Maurice 'Buck' Buckley continued to lead No. 75 (New Zealand) Squadron through most of 1940.

Already 45 years of age, he did not fly operationally with the squadron, but his logbook shows him continuing to train pilots from the captain's seat up until August. His wisdom and experience were more valuably employed in making better airmen, no doubt saving lives in the process, and his men performed admirably, achieving a good operational record with relatively low losses. But there was no lack of daring and the squadron's deeds would soon make their countrymen proud.

Squadron Leader 'Cyrus' Kay was awarded the squadron's first Distinguished Flying Cross (DFC) in June for a low-level attack on motorised troops sheltering in a forest. Then Sergeants 'Ted' Williams and Jim Carter were awarded the unit's first Distinguished Flying Medals (DFM) in July. Buckley himself received a Mention in Despatch from Portal in August. By the end of its first eight months of operations, the squadron had earned 12 DFCs and 12 DFMs. In that same period, it lost just five crews. It was a very happy squadron.

The Weekly News reported in November 1940:

> The Squadron's C.O. is Wing Commander M.W. Buckley of Fairlie, who is intensely proud of all his boys.
>
> 'He's the wizard of all C.O.'s,' [sic] said one of them. 'He looks after us just like a father. If ever we want anything we just go along to him and he gets it done in a quarter of the time anyone else would take. We call him "Old Buck" – but not to his face. He's a wizard bloke.'

Kay continued as Buckley's right-hand man and flight commander, he and his crew flying 22 operations. The citation to his DFC described one of them:

> This officer was captain of an aircraft ordered to attack important targets in the forests south of Bourlers and Baileux during a night in June. In spite of extremely difficult conditions, and in the face of severe opposition, he successfully bombed the objective, starting several fires which gave accurate direction to other aircraft of this sortie. He then descended to a low altitude and, again in the face of heavy opposition, attacked the woods with all his machine guns. Sqn. Ldr. Kay has conducted a number of operations in recent weeks and has shown daring, determination and outstanding ability.

After his tour had ended, Kay was presented with his DFC by the King at Buckingham Palace on 3 September and was posted out to Honington on the 23rd.

Buckley's term commanding the squadron came to an end in November and he was posted out to Stradishall on the 24th.

Kay was posted back in and promoted to wing commander the following day to assume command of 75 (NZ) Squadron. It was a seamless transition, Cyrus Kay's style of leadership was similar to Buckley's and he was already well-liked and well-respected by his men.

On 20 December, Buckley was back at Feltwell for a VIP visit by the governor-general-designate of New Zealand, Sir Cyril Newall, accompanied by Air Marshal Richard Peirse, the new head of Bomber Command (Portal had been promoted to Chief of Air Staff), and Air Vice-Marshal Jack Baldwin, Air Officer Commanding No. 3 Group. Newall was about to leave England to take up his new role in New Zealand; part of the visit involved a dinner and the presentation of two special paintings he was to take with him.

Wing Commander Maurice Buckley MBE RNZAF, Commanding Officer No. 75 (NZ) Squadron RAF, Feltwell, 1940. (M.W. Buckley collection)

One was *Return at Dawn* by Charles Cundall, showing Kay's Wellington and crew being welcomed back by Buckley from a night raid on Germany in July 1940. The squadron had commissioned the painting and raised £100 by subscription. The other painting was a portrait of Maurice Buckley by Oswald Birley. Both still hang in the Officers Mess at RNZAF Base Ohakea, alongside later Birley portraits of Wing Commander Cyril Kay and Sergeant James Ward VC.

On 1 March 1941, Buckley was appointed Station Commander, RAF Feltwell, and promoted to group captain on 1 April. Pleased to be back at Feltwell, he was able to watch over 'his' boys and continue to work on their behalf. His routine included waiting up for them to return from operations. After landing, crews would take off their kit in the crew room and often report briefly to Buckley before their debriefing with the intelligence officer.

> 'We may not have hit our target, we may have got lost, or everything may have gone off well, or we may have been badly knocked about,' said one of the pilots. 'Whatever has happened "Old Buck" always gives us a good welcome and makes us feel that we've done a good job. He always says to us, "Good show, good show!"'

One of the projects he worked on during this time was a badge and a motto for the unit. Correspondence with the College of Arms shows Buckley had suggested a badge based on a Kea (the native Alpine parrot) and the Maori motto 'Ake Ake Kia Kaha' (For ever and ever be strong).

On 2 July, however, all his plans and good works were rudely interrupted. Wallingford's successor as NZ Liaison Officer, Fred Newell, wrote to Buckley advising him he was to be recalled to New Zealand, as they were 'extremely short of experienced senior officers'. Buckley did not want to leave his post and he lobbied Bomber Command, the Air Ministry, and right up to New Zealand Prime Minister Peter Fraser, to stay on in England. It was even proposed Kay should be sent back instead. However, New Zealand would not budge and, in a letter from Newell on the 9th, Buckley was given 14 July as his date of release from Bomber Command. It would not have helped his mood that the role they envisaged for him back home was command of a Service Flying Training School.[1]

Buckley's attachment to his work, his squadron and his men is understandable, and the feeling would have been mutual. His leadership and role as 'father' of the squadron had become legendary, with 'Old Buck' featuring in several squadron songs and stories. In August 1941, just before he was posted back to New Zealand, Buckley once again paid his respects to those who had been with him from the beginning:

> During the present year the work of the squadron has gone on and its reputation for hard work has increased. We have been high up on the Bomber Command lists for efficiency and for the number of raids carried out and targets attacked. Our losses have been surprisingly few and I feel that in large measure this is due to the very careful work put in by that band of enthusiastic instructors I had in the early days, and by the foundations they laid.[2]

Baldwin wrote to him on 8 August:

> My dear Buck,
>
> I am very sorry to hear that in spite of your efforts and those of the Prime Minister the Government has insisted on your being sent back to New Zealand.
>
> I understand that they have asked for you to be made available by the 11th. I do hope you will be able to come and see me before you go.
>
> I am very sorry to lose you and can only thank you very much for all the excellent work you have put in, both as Squadron Commander and as a Station Commander. The record of Feltwell Station while you have been in Command has been unsurpassed by any in the Group, both with regard to successful operations carried out and the very high percentage of serviceability which your maintenance crews have managed to produce.
>
> All good luck to you in your new appointment.
>
> Yours sincerely
>
> Jack Baldwin.

Buckley replied to Baldwin on the 15th, thanking him sincerely and expressing his regret at having to leave the group, writing 'I consider that my work at Feltwell is not half completed'. He also acknowledged Baldwin's early support in the genesis of 75 (NZ) Squadron:

> I would like to take this opportunity of thanking you for all you have done for the New Zealanders in this Group, especially the small party I brought with me from Harwell to Stradishall. It was only after getting your words of encouragement and support that I realized we would be able to bring the N.Z. Unit intact to an Operational State.

Baldwin signed off Buckley's 1941 logbook:

> An excellent Squadron and Station Commander whose services I shall miss.

Meanwhile, Cyrus Kay had ended his term as commanding officer of 75 (NZ) Squadron and was posted out on 27 August.

It was the end of an era.

~ ~ ~ ~ ~ ~ ~ ~

With both Buckley and Kay gone, the leadership style at Feltwell changed significantly.

A new station commander was posted in, Group Captain John 'Speedy' Powell RAF, and then, surprisingly, an English commanding officer, Wing Commander Reginald Sawrey-Cookson DSO DFC. Sawrey-Cookson had served with the original 75 Squadron in 1937, and then under Powell at No. 149 Squadron.

From the day Powell arrived, he took a much more active role in day-to-day operations than his predecessor Buckley. His blunt style coincided with a new and controversial group policy to reduce bombing heights and increase bomb loads at the expense of petrol, sometimes with lethal consequences. There was a drop in squadron morale that took some time to recover.

Although its commanding officers and flight commanders were mostly New Zealanders through the war years, the squadron never achieved a full New Zealand complement. However, 'Number 75' went on to build its own unique and very successful 'Commonwealth' culture and identity, and a formidable reputation.

It ended the Second World War having flown the highest number of operational sorties of all the Royal Air Force's (RAF) heavy bomber squadrons, suffering the second-highest rate of aircraft operational losses in Bomber Command, and delivering the second-largest tonnage of bombs. Of the 1,320 New Zealand airmen who served with the squadron between 1940 and 1945, 519 lost their lives.

It was only in July 1945, when the European war was over and the squadron re-organised to train for the Far Eastern and Pacific Theatres, that it became fully New Zealand-manned. Tiger Force was the British Commonwealth long-range heavy bomber force set up for the invasion of Japan. After the surrender of Japan, plans for Tiger Force ended, however, and 75 (NZ) Squadron disbanded in October 1945.

In an unprecedented gesture of respect for the unit's wartime achievements, the RAF passed the squadron number, colours and battle honours to the Royal New Zealand Air Force (RNZAF) in 1946. No. 75 Squadron RNZAF would continue to uphold this proud heritage until its own disbandment on 13 December 2001.

~ ~ ~ ~ ~ ~ ~ ~

After a short six-month stint at the Air Ministry, Ralph Cochrane had been posted to RAF Abingdon as station commander. In April 1940, at the same time the original 75 Squadron gave up its numberplate and became No. 15 Operational Training Unit, the two squadrons based at Abingdon (Nos. 97 and 166) were disbanded and redesignated as No. 10 Operational Training Unit. This led to Cochrane's promotion to air commodore and command of No. 7 (Operational Training) Group in July 1940, and later his appointment by Air Chief Marshal Sir Charles Portal, by now Chief of the Air Staff, as Director of Flying Training at the Air Ministry. It was a crucial part of the RAF's war effort and Cochrane's term included the introduction of heavy conversion units for advanced heavy bomber crew training. He was made a Companion of the Order of the Bath in the 1943 New Year's Honours.

On 12 September 1942, Cochrane took over command of 3 Group from Air Vice-Marshal Baldwin. By now he was back working under Arthur 'Bomber' Harris, Air Officer Commanding-in-Chief, Bomber

Command. At 3 Group, he took a particular interest in 75 (NZ) Squadron, visiting the unit at Mildenhall on 23 October and Newmarket on 28 November.

In February 1943, Harris put him in charge of No. 5 Group, his best-known role, which included the establishment of No. 617 Squadron and overall command of Operation *Chastise*, the famous Dams raid in 1943, and of the series of attacks that resulted in the eventual sinking of the battleship *Tirpitz*. This also brought him back to work alongside his friend Barnes Wallis, who designed the bouncing bomb used by the Dam Busters, and later the 'Tallboy' and 'Grand Slam' bombs used by Nos. 9 and 617 Squadrons (albeit, the former did not carry the Grand Slam) to attack *Tirpitz* and various heavily fortified V-weapon, submarine, tunnel and rail targets in France and Germany. Innovations in target marking and bombing techniques were instrumental in 5 Group's many achievements under Cochrane's command. Harris described him at the time as 'in my view the best operational commander we have today' and later, in his book *Bomber Offensive*, 'a most brilliant, enthusiastic, hard-working leader of men'. Cochrane was appointed a Knight Commander of the Most Excellent Order of the British Empire in the 1945 New Year's Honours.

He moved to Transport Command in February 1945, promoted to acting air marshal. On an extensive tour of the command's network later that year, he stopped off briefly in New Zealand, met up with (now Air Commodore and Deputy Chief of the Air Staff) Maurice Buckley and was feted as guest of honour at a lunch hosted by Prime Minister Peter Fraser.

In August 1947, Cochrane was appointed Air Officer Commander-in-Chief, Flying Training Command. He was knighted with a KCB in 1948 and a GBE in 1950 and rose to the rank of Vice Chief of the Air Staff in the RAF before retiring in November 1952. Back in civilian life, Cochrane first joined the board of a new ship-building company, Atlantic, based at Newport, and then in 1956 moved to Rolls-Royce in Derby to head up a research department.

He visited New Zealand again in 1958, as guest of the New Zealand Government and the RNZAF, celebrating its 21st birthday. By now, Air Vice-Marshal Cyril Kay was Chief of the Air Staff and Cochrane was principal guest of honour at the 21st Anniversary RNZAF air pageant at Ohakea, and at a 75 (NZ) Squadron reunion held in nearby Palmerston North.

Cochrane retired from Rolls-Royce in 1961, became involved in several family businesses, and was a sought-after speaker and commentator on defence issues. He died at Burford, Oxfordshire, on 17 December 1977.

~~~~~~~~

After leaving 75 (NZ) Squadron, Cyrus Kay worked in an administrative role at 3 Group Headquarters, then served on the staff at No. 8 Group.

He returned to New Zealand with his wife and two daughters in late 1941 and continued his distinguished career with the RNZAF. He served as commanding officer at the RNZAF Navigation School at New Plymouth (1942–43), was promoted to group captain in March 1943, then served as base commander at, first, Ohakea (1943–44) then Wigram (1944–46).

After the war, he attended the Imperial Defence College, returning to New Zealand in 1947 with the new rank of air commodore to take up the position of Air Member for Supply. During this period, he briefly held the position of Acting Chief of the Air Staff. He was awarded the CBE in the 1948 New Year's Honours. In 1950, Kay was appointed Air Officer Commanding RNZAF Headquarters, London, arriving in December to take over the post from Maurice Buckley.

He returned to New Zealand in 1953 to take up the post of Air Member for Personnel. In May 1956, Kay led a goodwill mission to the United States and, on 5 June that year, was promoted to air vice-marshal and Chief of the Air Staff of the RNZAF. Through the 1950s, Kay played a leading role in rebuilding and reshaping the post-war, peacetime RNZAF, including the conversion of the RNZAF strike force to jets.

He was awarded the CBE in the New Year's Honours, 1958. This year was also the 21st anniversary of the establishment of the RNZAF and in February an impressive anniversary air show and Air Force Day was held at RNZAF Ohakea, with several friendly air forces participating. Kay hosted an array of VIPs, including the governor-general and acting prime minister, with Air Chief Marshal Sir Ralph Cochrane attending as special guest of honour.

To cap off an amazing career in aviation, one inspired by the travelling barnstormers, on 29 March 1958, Air Vice-Marshal Kay became the first New Zealander to break the sound barrier over home ground, in a USAF F-100 Super Sabre jet fighter. He retired on 30 June 1958.

Kay wrote his autobiography *The Restless Sky* in 1964.

As a former commanding officer, Kay was involved in the early activities of the 75 Squadron Association and attended reunions in New Zealand whenever he could. He travelled to England in 1978 for a joint UK–NZ Reunion at Cambridge and Mepal, where he was one of the guests of honour and was reunited with his 'old original' 2nd pilot, Eric Best, along with 'Popeye' Lucas and many other old friends.

Cyril Eyton Kay died in London on 29 April 1993.

~ ~ ~ ~ ~ ~ ~ ~

Maurice Buckley reluctantly returned to New Zealand with his family in November 1941 and immediately took up the role of Officer Commanding, RNZAF Station Whenuapai.

In November 1942, he was given command of the newly established Northern Group, RNZAF, responsible for the country's northern air defences and, on 1 April 1943, was promoted to air commodore. He served as aide-de-camp to the governor-general, Sir Cyril Newall, representing him at several formal events and accompanying him on a trip to forward bases in the Pacific Islands in November 1943.

Buckley was posted to the Pacific Theatre in January 1944 as Officer Commanding No. 1 (Islands) Group RNZAF, based at Guadalcanal and taking over the role from his old friend Air Commodore Sidney Wallingford. He returned to Wellington in November 1944 to take up the role of Deputy Chief of Staff, RNZAF. On 18 October 1945, at Rongotai, in recognition of his work in the Pacific, he was presented with the US Legion of Merit, Degree of Commander, by Rear Admiral Paul Hendren USN.

Buckley was awarded the CBE in the 1946 King's Birthday Honours and in May he and his family sailed for England again for him to take up the position of Air Officer Commanding RNZAF Headquarters in London and Air Liaison Officer. In that role, he was involved in the effort to locate and identify the remains of RNZAF airmen missing in Europe, and his wife Pat accompanied him on visits to war cemeteries across the Continent. His role also involved planning for post-war Commonwealth defence cooperation, including the purchase by the RNZAF of surplus RAF aircraft, in particular, 80 de Havilland Mosquitos.

These needed to be flown out to New Zealand and there was a nice historical symmetry when, in December 1946, plans were announced for Buckley, Ralph Cochrane and High Commissioner Bill Jordan to inspect the first ferry flight of ten Mosquitos before they flew out of RAF Pershore bound for New Zealand. Unfortunately, bad weather delayed take off and the arrangements fell through.

Air Commodore Maurice Buckley marched in the June 1946 Victory Parade in London and, together with Wing Commander Aubrey Breckon, represented the RNZAF at the Battle of Britain Chapel dedication at Westminster Abbey in July 1947. In October 1949, along with the Hon. Bill Jordan, he took part in a much more personal service, the unveiling and dedication of the Cross of Sacrifice in the service plot at Feltwell's St. Nicholas Churchyard.

Returning to New Zealand in 1950, Buckley retired from the RNZAF. The following year, he was contacted by a small group of 75 (NZ) Squadron veterans planning a first reunion, with a view to forming a squadron association. A very successful inaugural reunion was held in November 1951, with 'Buck' sitting as chairman. He was an enthusiastic supporter of the idea of an association and received a rapturous welcome from the 200 conference attendees.

The 75 Squadron Association was formed and, at the second reunion in May 1952, Buckley was elected as president and newly knighted Sir Bill Jordan appointed as patron. One of the items on the agenda was to fill in the many gaps in the squadron's written history and to put together a photographic record from members' private albums. A third reunion was held in 1954 and Buckley became the first recipient of the association's gold badge.

By the time the fourth reunion came around in May 1956, Buckley had been unwell for some time and had to send his apologies.

Maurice William 'Buck' Buckley died in Wellington on 3 November 1956.

~ ~ ~ ~ ~ ~ ~ ~

Foundation NZ Squadron members Joe White and 'Ted' Williams (above); Bill Steven, 'Popeye' Lucas and Dick Read (below), first 75 (NZ) Squadron Reunion, November 1951. (Alexander Turnbull Library)

Notes & References

1. Letters from NZLO S/L F. Newell to G/C M. Buckley, 2nd and 9th of July 1941, M.W. Buckley collection.

2. Suggested script for Group Captain Buckley's Broadcast to New Zealand, letter to H.L. Saunders, Air Ministry, 20th of August 1941, M.W. Buckley collection.

Buck's Treasure

If it wasn't for Maurice Buckley's efforts, the full story of the New Zealand Squadron would probably have been lost.

Disrupted and greatly overshadowed by the outbreak of war, the details of the ferry flight programme have been largely forgotten. The subsequent precarious transition from a single flight to an operational squadron took seven months but, again, many of the details have either been lost or mis-stated over the years.

'Buck' had the foresight to record or retain much of the historic material that passed through his hands. He kept or transcribed many documents that would have otherwise been lost, saved letters, cards and newspaper clippings, and from his time flying with the Royal Naval Air Service in 1916 onwards, assembled a priceless collection of photographs. Even a piece of the smashed propeller from the Sopwith 1½ Strutter he ditched in the Aegean Sea in July 1917 found its way back to New Zealand!

Following the war and his retirement from the RNZAF, his treasure trove was stored in his garage at the family home in Paekakariki. There are stories of individuals from the aviation community who were lucky enough to see it and were blown away by how much truly historic material there was. For example, he had kept the pencil-written notes on scraps of paper that were passed from wireless operator Tom McWilliams to co-pilot Charles Ulm (in the absence of an intercom) on the very first crossing of the Tasman in 1928 by Kingsford Smith's *Southern Cross*.

After Buck passed away, his wife Pat continued to organise, annotate and add to the collection. In 1966, she arranged for the most important material to be placed with the Alexander Turnbull Library. Other items were donated to Archives New Zealand and to various museums. Thankfully, the family continued to treasure the large stash that remained in the garage and almost all of Buck's original collection has survived.

The Archives New Zealand Buckley Collection was a revelation when I first got to look through it in 2016; there is a wealth of information from the time of the New Zealand Squadron, that murky period from May 1939 to March 1940 – from Buck's hand-written bombing-range notes to full squadron nominal rolls and a lengthy chain of correspondence relating to the formation of No. 75 (NZ) Squadron, even secret cypher messages from the New Zealand prime minister.

More gaps in our knowledge of that period were filled with information from Buck's log books (1937–43) and the Squadron Flight Authorisation Book, both held by the Air Force Museum of New Zealand at Wigram.

Then, in 2021, contact was made with the Buckley family, who still had in their possession four old, battered suitcases full of his photos, letters, medals and memorabilia. These contain even more information on the very early days of the New Zealand Squadron, some of it in Buck's own words and his wife Pat's beautiful handwriting.

The family are justifiably proud of Buck and his achievements. They are keen to keep his memory alive and to share his collection with the wider aviation community. This project has benefitted greatly from their generosity. Over a period of 12 months, starting with a very memorable and hospitable weekend in Gisborne, we worked our way through the suitcases and digitised each item. It was such a privilege to meet them, to see Buck's treasure firsthand, and to learn more about him and his amazing career.

Buck was a quiet, humble man whose huge contribution to New Zealand aviation is not widely known. The same could be said of 'Cyrus' Kay, Aubrey Breckon and several others from his team.

Hopefully this re-telling of the story of the New Zealand Squadron will help to at least partly rectify that.

Sources

'75 (NZ) Squadron', at https://75nzsquadron.wordpress.com.

Album presented to W. J. Jordan – PH-ALB-522-1, Auckland War Memorial Museum.

Auckland War Memorial Museum Online Cenotaph, at www.aucklandmuseum.com/war-memorial/online-cenotaph (various entries).

Baber, Flight Lieutenant T.J.D., RNZAF, personal diaries, via Dave Homewood.

Bomber Command History Form 78 Aircraft Movement Cards, at www.lancasterbombers.net/form-78-aircraft-movement-cards-2-2/form-78-vickers-wellington/.

Bond, Steve, *Wimpy: A Detailed Illustrated History of the Vickers Wellington in service, 1938–1953* Grub Street, London, 2014.

Buckley, Maurice William, private collection, Buckley family.

Caird, Felicity, 'The Strategic Significance of the Pacific Islands in New Zealand's Defence Policy, 1935–1939', published thesis, University of Canterbury, 1987.

Chapman, Peter, 'Naval Pilot in the Aegean', *The 14–18 Journal*, Australian Society of World War I Aero Historians, 1995 issue, p.21-29.

Cochrane, R.A., Report on the air aspect of the defence problems of New Zealand, including the suggested duties, strength and organization of the New Zealand Air Force, December 1936, 1. 102/4/1, National Archives of New Zealand and National Library of New Zealand: https://natlib.govt.nz/records/39032188

Cochrane, Ralph Alexander, papers relating to his time in New Zealand, Acc nos. 83/207 and 86/111, Air Force Museum of New Zealand.

Delve, Ken, *Vickers-Armstrongs Wellington*, Crowood Press Ltd, Wiltshire, 1998.

DSIR [Department of Scientific and Industrial Research] World War 2 Narratives. No 3. Radar. Copy No. 3, Reference: AAOQ 28051 W3424 16/, Archives New Zealand.

Duxbury, David, personal communications.

Franks, Norman, *Forever Strong: The Story of 75 Squadron RNZAF, 1916–1990*, Random Century, Auckland, New Zealand, 1991.

Hancock, Kenneth R., *New Zealand at War*, Reed, Wellington, 1946.

Hanson, C.M., *By Such Deeds : honours and awards in the Royal New Zealand Air Force, 1923–1999* Volplane Press, Christchurch, New Zealand, 2001.

Harris, Mary, *Rocks, radio and radar: the extraordinary scientific, social and military life of Elizabeth Alexander* World Scientific Publishing Europe Ltd, London, 2019.

Hewson, Brian J., *Goliath's Apprentice : The Royal New Zealand Air Force and the United States in the Pacific Air War 1941-1945*, published thesis, 2012.

Homewood, Dave, personal communications.

Imperial War Museum online photographic collections, at www.iwm.org.uk/collections/photographs.

Kay, Cyril Eyton, *The Restless Sky*, Harrap, London, 1964.

Lockstone, Brian, *Into Wind ... The birth of the RNZAF*, RNZAF Museum, Christchurch, 2007.

Lucas, Lorie, *Popeye's War: a biography of Wing Commander F.J. Lucas*, L.J. Lucas, Motueka, New Zealand, 1996.

Macfarlane AFC, S/L R.C., *A History of No 75 Squadron, RNZAF*, Part II, Chapter 1 (1937–1940), 75 Squadron RAF/RNZAF Association.

Martyn, Errol, personal communications.

Martyn, Errol W., *For Your Tomorrow : A record of New Zealanders who have died while serving with the RNZAF and Allied Air Services since 1915 – Volume 3: Biographies & Appendices*, Volplane Press, Christchurch, 2008.

McIntyre, W. David, *New Zealand Prepares for War: Defence Policy, 1919–39*, University of Canterbury Press, 1988.

Mead, Richard, *Dambuster-in-Chief: The Life of Air Chief Marshal Sir Ralph Cochrane*, Pen & Sword Aviation, Yorkshire, 2020.

M.W. Buckley logbooks, ref 2017/069.4 and 2017/069.5; T.O. Freeman and A.A.N. Breckon personal photo albums, Air Force Museum of New Zealand.

M.W. Buckley collection – ADQA 17358 AIR167/2/4 Part 3 – Unregistered file – Wing Commander [later Air Commodore] M.W. Buckley – personal file – officers, June 1939 – July 1941 and Defence of NZ – General – Report on meeting held in Mr Berendsen's Room (Address by Dr Martyn) – 28/7/39, Archway Item ID:R18871379, Archives New Zealand.

New Zealand contracts for Wellingtons, 1938–1951, GBR/0012/MS Vickers Doc 403, Cambridge University Library.

New Zealand Squadron Flight Authorisation Book, Air Force Museum of New Zealand.

No. 75 (NZ) Squadron Operations Record Book, R.A.F. Forms 540 & 541, March – May 1940, Ref: AIR/27/645/, The National Archives (UK).

O'Connor, Derek, 'Flight of the Wellesleys', *HistoryNet*, at www.historynet.com/flight-of-the-wellesleys/.

Report by the Honourable F. Jones, Minister in Charge of the Air Department, for the Year Ended 31st of March 1939, NZ Government, Appendices to the Journals of House of Representatives (and the Votes & Proceedings), 'Papers Past' Parliamentary Papers, National Library of New Zealand, at https://paperspast.natlib.govt.nz/parliamentary/AJHR1939-I.2.3.2.42.

Ross, J.M.S., *Royal New Zealand Air Force*, War History Branch, Dept. of Internal Affairs, Wellington, New Zealand, 1955.

Saunders, Hilary St. George, *Return at Dawn: The Official History of the New Zealand Bomber Squadron of the RAF from June, 1939 to July, 1942*, Director of Publicity, Wellington, New Zealand, 1942.

Spencer, Alex M., *British Imperial Air Power: The Royal Air Forces and the Defense of Australia and New Zealand Between the World Wars*, Purdue University Press, West Lafayette, Indiana, 2020.

The Bold Have Wings, radio documentary, Ngā Taonga Sound & Vision, 1958, at www.ngataonga.org.nz/search-use-collection/search/29969/.

Turner, Chas. Wm., *Reinforced Concrete Hangars for Air Force Stations in New Zealand, Proceedings*, Vol. XXXIV, New Zealand Institution of Engineers, 1948.

Vickers Wellington – The Backbone of Bomber Command, Key Publishing, 2013.

Ward, Chris and Chris Newey, *75 (NZ) Squadron*, Mention The War Publications, Farsley, Pudsey, 2018.

Wilson, Andrew, personal communications, Brooklands Museum.

Wood, F.L.W., *Political and External Affairs, The Official History of New Zealand in the Second World War 1939–1945*, Historical Publications Branch, 1958, online publication, New Zealand Electronic Text Collection, Victoria University of Wellington, accessed 2016, at https://ndhadeliver.natlib.govt.nz/webarchive/20210104000423/http://nzetc.victoria.ac.nz/tm/scholarly/tei-WH2Poli.html.

Acknowledgements

A very special thanks to the Buckley family for access to the magnificent MW Buckley collection and permission to reproduce records and photographs. Buck's account and the documents he kept were crucial to the telling of this story.

A special and very grateful thank you to Matthew O'Sullivan, Simon Moody and the Air Force Museum of New Zealand for their generous assistance and permission to reproduce photographs, for access to key logbooks and for access to the New Zealand Squadron's Flight Authorisation Book.

Thanks to Andrew Wilson, Beatrice Meecham and Andrew Lewis at Brooklands Museum and Julian Temple, Heritage Archivist, BAE Systems.

Thanks to Heidi Domeisen, Anna Rhodes-Sayer, Kerry Foster, Ian Carswell, Mick West and Andy Thomas for sourcing photographs and information, and thanks to Heidi and Anna for information on the fate of the John Collins crew.

Thanks to the Lucas family for access to the FJ 'Popeye' Lucas collection and permission to reproduce photographs.

Thanks to Errol Martyn for his generous help, expertise and incomparable knowledge of New Zealand aviation history.

Thanks to Andy Wright for his encouragement, patience, advice and expertise.

Thanks to Ian Campbell for his advice and assistance.

Thanks also to Dave Homewood for his efforts in keeping RNZAF history alive via his 'Wings Over New Zealand' forum, website, meetings, podcasts and recorded interviews. Also for access to the personal diaries of Flight Lieutenant TJD Baber RNZAF. This project owes a lot to our conversations and debates over several years, and to Dave's help and encouragement.

Thanks to the New Zealand Bomber Command Association, and in particular to Peter Wheeler for his outstanding efforts in preserving veterans' photographs, documents and stories, honouring their lives and making sure we will not forget them.

Thanks to Dom Howard, Bomber Command History, for making his extensive archive of aircraft records freely available to researchers.

www.75nzsquadron.com: Special thanks to Simon Sommerville for his colossal personal effort to keep the memories of the boys of No. 75 (NZ) Squadron alive through his website, collections, records and databases of aircraft, airmen and their individual histories. Simon very generously helped me get started on my research journey and has been a regular source of inspiration.

Appendices

1. New Zealand Squadron personnel, May 1939 – April 1940
2. List of 1st Mobile Flight personnel
3. List of 2nd – 4th Mobile Flights personnel
4. The NZ Wellingtons

Appendix 1

New Zealand Squadron personnel, May 1939 – 4 April 1940

Rank given is the highest held while serving with the New Zealand Squadron.

Abbs, Corporal SG, RAF 562426
Fitter I
Foundation member, June 1939
Ground role, did not fly operations
Awarded MiD 11.3.41

Adams, Aircraftman Gilbert Ernest, RAF 632805
Wireless Operator/Air Gunner
Posted in 13.11.39
Flew 11 operations with 75 (NZ) Squadron: two as front gunner with the CE Kay crew and nine as rear gunner with the FJ Lucas crew. Promoted to sergeant, circa 10.6.40. Absent from operations in June and flew only one more, in July.
Posted out ca. August 1940. Later with 625 Squadron.

Adams, Flying Officer John 'Jack', RNZAF NZ1027
Pilot. Nominated pilot for the 1st Mobile Flight.
Foundation member, July 1939
A New Zealander in the RAF, he obtained a short-service commission in the RAF on 8.3.37 and flew Whitleys. Transferred to the RNZAF 10.7.39 on posting to the New Zealand Squadron. Listed as squadron adjutant when the squadron moved to Feltwell, 1.2.40
Flew 35 operations with 75 (NZ) Squadron (including six DNC) with his own crew. Awarded DFC 22.10.40.
Posted out 12.1.41. No. 5 BATF. Awarded AFC 1.1.42. Flew with Atlantic Ferry and RAF Transport Command. Returned to New Zealand. Wing commander and CO, 40 Squadron RNZAF (Dakota, Hudson, Lodestar) June 1943 – November 1944 (taking over from S/L 'Popeye' Lucas). Flew an RAF Transport Command Skymaster from the UK to NZ in December 1945 and a Lancastrian in March 1946, in record time. Died 8.10.95.

Albert, Aircraftman Eric Norman, RAF 623339
Wireless Operator/Air Gunner
Posted in 13.11.39
Flew 29 operations with 75 (NZ) Squadron: two as front gunner with the AAN Breckon crew, 19 as front gunner and as wireless operator with the CE Kay crew, one each as wireless operator for the TO Freeman, FJ Lucas, JC Fleming and CK Saxelby crews, and four as wireless operator with the MH Macfarlane crew.
Posted out 11.40. Awarded DFM 11.2.41.
Posted in unknown date for second tour

Allen, Aircraftman V, RAF 563321
Flight Mechanic
Ground role, did not fly operations

Allinson, Sergeant William Alfred, RAF 526281
Observer

Posted in 13.11.39

Flew 33 operations with 75 (NZ) Squadron (including five DNC) as observer with the J Adams crew. Posted out September 1940. Awarded DFM 22.10.40. Received commission 7.8.41 (46307). Later flight lieutenant and DFC with 140 Squadron.

Anderson, Leading Aircraftman Ronald Alexander John, RNZAF NZ36139

Wireless Operator. Nominated crew member for the 1st Mobile Flight.

Foundation member, July 1939

One of the six wireless specialists, trained at the RNZAF's new Wireless School at Wigram, sent to England in January 1939 to train for the New Zealand Squadron ferry flights with Wellington squadrons in the RAF. Served with 99 Squadron. Posted to the New Zealand Squadron in July 1939. Flew 12 operations with 75 (NZ) Squadron: two as wireless operator with the CE Kay crew and ten with the SMM Watson crew. Promoted to sergeant prior to commencing operations. Promoted to flight sergeant, circa 10.7.40.

Lost with the Watson crew 20.7.40 during a raid on Horst, Germany, his 11th operation with that crew, age 26. Next of kin Mrs Anderson (mother), Northamptonshire, England. Buried Reichswald Forest War Cemetery, Germany.

Armstrong, Leading Aircraftman Albert James, RAF 527280

Flight Rigger

Foundation member, June 1939

Ground role, did not fly operations

Awarded MiD 11.3.41

Bloor, Aircraftman William Henry, RAF 616118

Flight Rigger

Posted in unknown date

Ground role, did not fly operations

Breckon, Flight Lieutenant Aubrey Arthur Ninnis 'Breck', RNZAF NZ1025 (70016)/RAF 37539

Pilot. Nominated pilot for the 1st Mobile Flight.

Foundation member, 17.6.39. Photographic specialist.

Pre-war, he had been a photographer for the New Zealand Herald and the Auckland Weekly News. A New Zealander in the RAF, he obtained a short-service commission in the RAF in November 1935 and flew Heyfords and Whitleys with 10 Squadron, Dishforth. Transferred to the RNZAF 17.6.39 on posting to the New Zealand Squadron. Listed as photographic officer when the squadron moved to Feltwell, 1.2.40.

Flew 33 operations with 75 (NZ) Squadron (including three DNC), a highlight being the epic 14-hour Narvik, Norway, reconnaissance flight of 12.4.40. Promoted to squadron leader and flight commander 'B' Flight 5.8.40, after the death of Squadron Leader WI Collett. Awarded DFC 13.9.40.

Posted out 9.9.40 to 11 Operational Training Unit, Bassingbourn. Returned to New Zealand in June 1941. CO, RNZAF Ashburton. CO, NZ Pacific Ferry, Ford Island, Hawaii, ferrying Ventura aircraft to New Zealand, May 1943 – May 1944. Wing commander and CO, 1 Squadron RNZAF (Ventura) February – June 1945. CO, RNZAF Field HQ, Emirau. CO, RNZAF Mechanics Bay. Together with Air Commodore Maurice Buckley, represented the RNZAF at the Battle of Britain Chapel dedication, Westminster Abbey, London, July 1947. Senior Air Staff Officer RNZAF HQ, London. RAF Staff College, Bracknell. OC Flying, 75 Squadron RNZAF, Ohakea, from February 1950. Later group captain. His younger brother Ivan also served with 75 (NZ) Squadron. Died 1.4.89.

Brooks, Aircraftman John Stanley 'Stan', RAF 622115

Wireless Operator/Air Gunner

Posted in 13.11.39

Flew six operations with 75 (NZ) Squadron as wireless operator with the JN Collins crew.

Shot down 21/22.5.40 on his sixth operation with the Collins crew near Tournai, Belgium. Both pilots killed but the rest of the crew baled out, landed in the middle of a battle zone and were immediately captured. Brooks, rear gunner Hockey and observer Thorpe were the squadron's first POWs. PoW #50392. Promoted to sergeant then warrant officer. Safe UK, date unknown. Later Secretary of the Friends of the 75 Squadron Association UK. Awarded MBE for his services.

Brown, Sergeant Norman Wilson, RAF 518807

Observer

Posted in 13.11.39

Flew 26 operations with 75 (NZ) Squadron as observer with the WH Coleman crew. Awarded DFM 13.9.40.

Lost on his 26th operation with all the Coleman crew, near Amsterdam, returning from Kassel, 26.7.40. Age 24, son of Arthur Kinnear Brown and Ethel Brown, of Hull; husband of Minnie Brown, of Hull. Buried Amsterdam New Eastern Cemetery, Netherlands.

Buckley, Wing Commander Maurice William 'Buck', RNZAF NZ1005

Pilot. Officer Commanding New Zealand Squadron. Commanding officer and pilot, 1st Mobile Flight. Foundation member, May 1939.

Served in First World War as a pilot in the RNAS and RAF (scout, bomber, aerial reconnaissance and photography). Prominent in early commercial aviation in New Zealand, joined the NZ Permanent Air Force in 1926. Chief flying instructor, Sockburn, then CO, Wigram. Awarded MBE for services to the RNZAF in 1935. Squadron leader and Officer Commanding RNZAF Hobsonville. RAF exchange posting to England in 1937, with 97 and 116 Squadrons (Heyfords) and flight commander with 38 Squadron (Wellington). Established and led the New Zealand Squadron, Marham. Promoted to wing commander 10.11.39. Officer Commanding 75 (NZ) Squadron 4.4.40. No operations flown but continued in pilot-training role. Awarded MiD 31.8.40.

Posted out 24.11.40. Station Commander RAF Feltwell. Returned to New Zealand, November 1941. Officer Commanding RNZAF Whenuapai. Air Commodore and Officer Commanding Northern Group RNZAF. Officer Commanding 1 (Islands) Group RNZAF, January 1944. Deputy Chief of Staff, RNZAF, November 1944. Awarded the US Legion of Merit in October 1945. Air Officer Commanding RNZAF Headquarters in London and awarded CBE in 1946. Together with Wing Commander Aubrey Breckon, represented the RNZAF at the Battle of Britain Chapel dedication, Westminster Abbey, London, July 1947. Retired from the RNZAF in 1950. Died in 1956.

Burton, Leading Aircraftman A, RAF 402853

Armourer

On attachment from RAF Abingdon

Ground role, did not fly operations

Posted out before 20.1.40

Bussey, Leading Aircraftman Benjamin William, RAF 531682

Flight Rigger

Foundation member, June 1939

Ground role, did not fly operations

Joined the RAF in 1936. Worked on Handley Page Heyfords at Mildenhall and then Handley Page Harrows at Marham with 115 Squadron. Posted to the New Zealand Squadron in June 1939. Awarded MiD 25.9.41 for rescuing a trapped fellow ground crew member from the front turret of Wellington R1020 which had lost hydraulics and, on landing at Feltwell, on 18 November 1940, crashed into an armoured car and caught fire.

Campion, Leading Aircraftman John Joseph, RAF 536460
Electrician/Flight Rigger
Foundation member, June 1939
Ground role, did not fly operations
Awarded MiD 11.3.41

Carter, Sergeant Jim Whitelaw, RAF 527740
Observer
Posted in 13.11.39
Flew 23 operations with 75 (NZ) Squadron (including two DNC): 22 as observer with the CE Kay crew and one as observer with the JC Fleming crew. Awarded DFM 30.7.40.
Posted out November 1940

Charles, Pilot Officer Alfred Basil, RAFVR 76005
Air Gunner. Squadron Gunnery Officer.
Posted in early January 1940
Flew 13 operations with 75 (NZ) Squadron: 12 as rear gunner with the CE Kay crew and one as rear gunner with the FJ Lucas crew.
Posted out 29.9.40 to Parnall Armament School, Yate. Later squadron leader and MBE.

Clark, Aircraftman AE, RAF 614247
Flight Rigger
Foundation member, June 1939

Cohen, Squadron Leader Ronald Joseph 'Nugget', RNZAF NZ1015 (70005)
Pilot. Nominated as commanding officer, 2nd Mobile Flight.
Served a short-service commission in the RAF from 15.8.29 to 18.4.34, returned to New Zealand in 1935. Joined the RNZAF 29.6.35. Flight commander at RNZAF Hobsonville operating seaplanes. Officer in Command, Advanced Training Flight, RNZAF Wigram. Selected to travel to England to take up the position of flight commander with the New Zealand Squadron. Posted in mid-August 1939. Posted out January 1940, recalled to New Zealand. Officer in Command, Advanced Training Squadron, 2 Flying Training School, Blenheim, 1.41 – 5.42. Awarded AFC 1.1.41. AOC 1 (Islands) Group. Deputy Chief of the Air Staff, 1947. Attached to the RAF in 1948, group captain and Senior Air Staff Officer Advanced Headquarters, 46 Group, controlling operations of the RAF and civil transport force employed on the Berlin Airlift, June 1948 – April 1949. Awarded CBE 1.1.50 and also awarded US Legion of Merit that year, both for his efforts in the Berlin Airlift. Deputy Chief of the Air Staff, 1950–53. AOC Task Force Admin HQ, Inspector-General RNZAF, 1954. Died 28.6.95.

Colbourn, Sergeant Rupert Percy Frank, RAF 564590
Instrument Maker. Nominated crew member for the 1st Mobile Flight.
Foundation member, June 1939
Ground role, did not fly operations

Coleman, Pilot Officer William Harcourt 'Bill', RNZAF NZ2526/RAF39781
Pilot. Nominated pilot for the 1st Mobile Flight.
Foundation member, 7 July 1939
A New Zealander in the RAF. From Devonport but grew up in Christchurch and learned to fly at the Christchurch Gliding Club and then at the Auckland Aero Club, Mangere. Sailed to England, obtaining a short-service commission in the RAF, 5.4.37. Served with 97 Squadron on Heyfords and Whitleys, then briefly from January 1939 with 116 Squadron on Heyfords. Transferred to the RNZAF 7.7.39 on posting to the New Zealand Squadron.
Flew 29 operations with 75 (NZ) Squadron. Awarded DFC 22.10.40.

Lost on his 29th operation with all crew when their Wellington (probably damaged by anti-aircraft fire) crashed into the Ijsselmeer, the inland sea near Amsterdam, returning from Kassel, 26.7.40. Age 23. Next of kin, mother Mrs CM Walton, Devonport. Buried Amsterdam New Eastern Cemetery, Netherlands.

Collett, Flight Lieutenant Wilfred Ira, RAF 43232
Pilot

A New Zealander in the RAF, Collett had learned to fly in New Zealand at the Hawke's Bay Aero Club. He sailed to England in 1933 and joined the RAF in June 1934, serving in Egypt, the Middle East, Cyprus, and the North-West Frontier of India. In August 1939, he was posted to 38 Squadron on Wellingtons.

Attached briefly to the New Zealand Squadron while with 38 Squadron, October 1939. Collett flew 16 times with the squadron that month, initially dual training and practice flights with S/L Buckley as captain and instructor. Posted to 149 Squadron 16.2.40.

AVM Jack Baldwin mentions him in a letter to Buckley on 31 March 1940: 'In this respect, there is a New Zealander, Acting Squadron Leader Collett, who I believe would like to come to you and you might like to have him as your second Flight Commander as and when you feel prepared to form this flight.'

Posted in to 75 (NZ) Squadron on 5 May 1940 as squadron leader and inaugural flight commander of 'B' Flight.

Flew 18 operations with 75 (NZ) Squadron (including three DNC).

Died on 4 August 1940 of injuries received earlier that day on his 18th operation. On return from an attack on Gelsenkirchen, his Wellington badly shot-up and with a dead engine, Collett and crew had been diverted from Feltwell to Mildenhall. While attempting a wheels-up crash landing they ran into a fog bank and flew into a ridge at Barton Mills. The aircraft caught fire and three of the crew were injured, Collett seriously.

Age 28. Son of Edgar Arnold and Louise Amy Collett, of Gisborne, New Zealand; husband of Doreen Williamson Collett, of Gisborne. Buried at Feltwell (St. Nicholas) Churchyard, Norfolk, England.

Collins, Pilot Officer John Noel, RNZAF NZ2513
Pilot. Nominated pilot for the 1st Mobile Flight.
Foundation member, 5 July 1939

A New Zealander in the RAF, he had travelled to England and obtained a short-service commission in the RAF in 1937 and flew Blenheims with 104 Squadron. Transferred to the RNZAF 5.7.39 on posting to the New Zealand Squadron. Listed as signals officer when the squadron moved to Feltwell, 1.2.40.

Flew 11 operations with 75 (NZ) Squadron. Promoted to flight lieutenant 4.5.40.

Lost on his 11th operation on 21/22.5.40 when Wellington exploded after being hit by anti-aircraft fire and catching fire near Tournai, Belgium. Age 23. The squadron's first loss, the first RNZAF pilot to be killed while serving abroad in the Second World War and the first of the 12 original pilots to be lost. His 2nd pilot, Frank Sparling, was also killed, the rest of the crew were captured. Next of kin, father, Bertram Reginald Collins, Remuera. Believed to be buried in an un-named grave at Froyennes marked 'An Airman of the 1939-45 War - RAF - 21st May 1940. A Man Known only to God'. Commemorated on the Runnymede Memorial.

Colville, Corporal A, RAF
Fitter. Nominated crew member for the 1st Mobile Flight.
Foundation member, June 1939
Posted out some time before January 1940

Cross, Pilot Officer Ian Kingston Pembroke, RAF 39305
Pilot. Attached from 38 Squadron, Marham, May 1939.
Logged 0.50hrs flying with the New Zealand Squadron in May 1939.

Flew 34 operations with 38 Squadron, the first to Heligoland on 3.12.39, and one in which his aircraft ran out of petrol and the crew had to bale out. Posted to 11 Operational Training Unit as an instructor. Awarded DFC 13.9.40. Posted to 103 Squadron (Wellington) and flew 16 operations. Promoted to squadron leader, his aircraft was hit by anti-aircraft fire from German naval units on 12.2.42 (during the 'Channel Dash') and he had to ditch 40 miles off Rotterdam, two of his crew drowning. Rescued a day later and POW. One of the organisers of the 'Great Escape' at Stalag Luft III and leader of the 'Penguin' sand-disposal team. One of the 76 escapers on the night of 24/25.3.44. Caught and one of 50 escapers executed by the Gestapo, 31.3.44, age 25. Awarded posthumous MiD 8.6.44. Buried at Poznan Old Garrison Cemetery, Poland.

Curtis, Pilot Officer Richard Melville 'Dick', RAF 42200
Pilot
Posted in 9.12.39. Does not appear to have made any flights with the New Zealand Squadron. Obtained his 1st Pilot (Day) rating on Wellingtons from Maurice Buckley on 9.3.40.
Posted out 9.3.40 to 214 Squadron, Stradishall. This unit was not yet operational, so it is presumed he was still undergoing training.
Posted in 6.4.40 (now 75 (NZ) Squadron)
First flying practice 16.4.40; first operation 15.5.40.
Flew 30 operations with 75 (NZ) Squadron (including one DNC); 15 as 2nd pilot with the FJ Lucas crew (including one DNC) and 15 with his own crew. Received short-service commission 18.6.40. Awarded DFC 11.2.41.
Posted out 10.10.40 to 20 Operational Training Unit, Lossiemouth. To 2 School of Air Navigation (SAN), Cranage, 11.8.41. RAF College, Cranwell, 27.9.41. 1 SAN, Port Albert, Canada, 16.7.42. HQ Army Co-operation Command, 17.12.42. HQ Fighter Command, 2.6.43. HQ IXth American Air Force, 28.12.43.

Daly, Aircraftman Charles Oliver, RAF 632523
Aircraft Hand
Posted in unknown date
Ground role, did not fly operations

Day, Aircraftman Douglas Reginald 'Reg', RAF 632887
Wireless Operator/Air Gunner
Posted in 13.11.39
Also nicknamed 'Diz'
Flew 11 operations with 75 (NZ) Squadron: nine as front gunner and rear gunner with the J Adams crew, one as wireless operator with the AGL Humphries crew, and one as wireless operator with the RP Elliott crew.
Posted out unknown date

Dowds, Aircraftman John, RAF 632780
Wireless Operator/Air Gunner
Posted in 13.11.39
Flew 11 operations with 75 (NZ) Squadron as front gunner and rear gunner with the WH Coleman crew.
Lost on his 11th operation with the Coleman crew, near Amsterdam, returning from Kassel, age 23, 26.7.40. Son of Mr and Mrs D. Dowds, of Musselburgh, Midlothian. Buried Amsterdam New Eastern Cemetery, Netherlands.

Edwards, Aircraftman Arthur, RAF 629947
Wireless Operator/Air Gunner
Posted in 13.11.39

Flew three operations with 75 (NZ) Squadron: two as wireless operator with the WH Coleman crew and one with the JN Collins crew.
Posted out 20.4.40

Edwards, Leading Aircraftman Humphrey Hepburn, RAF 614709
Flight Rigger
Foundation member, June 1939
Ground role, did not fly operations

Ellis, Sergeant Robert John, RAF 519443
Observer
Posted in 13.11.39
Flew 29 operations with 75 (NZ) Squadron as observer with the WMC Williams crew. Awarded DFM 22.11.40.
Posted out August 1940

Emery, Leading Aircraftman Albert Eric, RAF 518344
Wireless Radio Mechanic/Flight Mechanic. Nominated crew member for the 1st Mobile Flight.
Foundation member, June 1939
Ground role, did not fly operations

Fairfax, Leading Aircraftman Ivan Donald, RAF 539770
Flight Rigger
Foundation member, June 1939
Ground role, did not fly operations

Flegg, Leading Aircraftman Harry James, RAF 617755
Flight Mechanic
Foundation member, June 1939
Ground role, did not fly operations

Freeman, Pilot Officer Trevor Owen, RAF/RNZAF NZ1026
Pilot. Nominated pilot for the 1st Mobile Flight.
Foundation member, 17.7.39
A New Zealander in the RAF, he learned to fly at the Otago Aero Club, then took up a short-service commission with the RAF 6.1.36, flying Gauntlets and Spitfires with 74 Squadron. Transferred to the RNZAF after posting to the New Zealand Squadron, 17.7.39. Listed as navigation officer when the squadron moved to Feltwell, 1.2.40.
Flew 31 operations with 75 (NZ) Squadron: three as 2nd pilot with the CE Kay crew, and 28 with own crew. Awarded DFC 22.10.40.
Posted out to RAF Station Feltwell 26.8.40. 3 Group training, 57 Squadron. Then wing commander and OC, 115 Squadron, 23.8.41. Awarded DSO 22.12.41. Awarded a Bar to DFC 4.8.42. Returned to New Zealand in March 1943 and posted to Director of Air Operations, RNZAF. Officer Commanding, RNZAF Fighter Wing, Ondonga, New Georgia Group, Solomon Islands.
Killed 17.12.43 near Rabaul leading a formation of 14 Squadron Kittyhawk fighters and credited with shooting down one Japanese 'Zero' before (probably) being shot down in combat with four others. No trace of him or his aircraft was ever found. Age 27, son of William Frederick and Eliza Allon Freeman, of Dunedin, Otago, New Zealand; husband of Judith Freeman. Commemorated on the Bourail Memorial, Bourail New Zealand War Cemetery, New Caledonia.

Frost, Flying Officer RAF
Squadron Engineering Officer (at Harwell, September 1939, possibly attached from 38 Squadron)

Garrard, Aircraftman Sidney Roy, RAF 631153
Wireless Operator/Air Gunner
Posted in 13.11.39
Flew 31 operations with 75 (NZ) Squadron as wireless operator with the WMC Williams crew. Awarded DFM 10.1.41
Posted out September 1940. Awarded MiD 17.3.41. Posted to 115 Squadron, 4.11.42, pilot officer.

Gethings, LAC Sidney, RAF 615742
Flight Rigger
Foundation member, June 1939
Ground role, did not fly operations

Gibb, Aircraftman John Webster, RAF 632040
Wireless Operator/Air Gunner
Posted in 13.11.39
Flew 24 operations with 75 (NZ) Squadron: four as rear gunner with the JN Collins crew, eight as front and rear gunner with the N Williams crew, four as rear gunner and front gunner with the CE Kay crew, one as rear gunner with the TO Freeman crew, and seven as wireless operator with the G Wright crew.
Posted out December 1940

Gibbs, Aircraftman Jack, RAF 625697
Wireless Operator/Air Gunner
Posted in 13.11.39
Flew 30 operations with 75 (NZ) Squadron: 26 as front and rear gunner with the J Adams crew, one as rear gunner with the AAN Breckon crew, and three as wireless operator with the RM Sanderson crew. Lost without trace on his 30th operation with the Sanderson crew, returning from Berlin 24.10.40. Age 19, son of Philip Frederick and Maud Beatrice Gibbs, of Newbold, Warwickshire. Commemorated on the Runnymede Memorial.

Gordon, Sergeant Alexander Duff, RAF 564496
Wireless and Electrical Mechanic. Nominated crew member for the 1st Mobile Flight.
Foundation member, June 1939
Ground role, did not fly operations
Awarded BEM 11.3.41

Gough, Aircraftman Albert, RAF 549484
Aircraft Hand
Posted in unknown date
Ground role, did not fly operations

Gow, Pilot Officer Ian Ronald, RAF 40820 / RNZAF NZ2215
Pilot
Posted in 1.3.40
A New Zealander in the RAF. Flew 26 operations with 75 (NZ) Squadron: 14 as 2nd pilot with the WH Coleman crew and 12 operations with own crew.
Posted out 25.1.41. Flight lieutenant 1.8.41. Squadron leader 1.6.44. Later wing commander, Air Defence Commander, 2 ADHQ, Wellington.

Green, Aircraftman Francis William 'Frank', RAF 581283
Wireless Operator/Observer
Posted in January 1940
Flew 30 operations with 75 (NZ) Squadron as observer with the FJ Lucas crew
Posted out November 1940

Posted in ca. July 1941 for second tour. Flew 13 operations as an observer with the FJ Lucas crew on Popeye's second tour. Awarded DFM 11.2.41. Posted out 21.5.42.

Green, Aircraftman Geoffrey, RAF 628871
Wireless Operator/Air Gunner
Posted in 13.11.39
Flew 30 operations with 75 (NZ) Squadron: five as wireless operator with the WH Coleman crew, ten as wireless operator with the JN Collins crew, and 15 as wireless operator with the EV Best crew. Posted out ca. October 1940. Lost with all crew, 70 Squadron Wellington crashed into a hill near Danilovograd, Yugoslavia, 18.11.40. Buried at Belgrade War Cemetery, Serbia.

Greenaway, Flight Lieutenant Arthur Beale, RNZAF NZ1034 (70015)/RAF 37802
Pilot. Nominated pilot for the 1st Mobile Flight.
Foundation member, June 1939
A New Zealander in the RAF, he obtained his civil 'A' pilot's licence in 1933. After serving with the NZAF March–December 1935, he obtained a short-service commission in the RAF 9.3.36 and flew fighters with 23 Squadron (Demon), Biggin Hill. Transferred to the RNZAF 29.8.38 and was posted to the New Zealand Squadron in June 1939.
Listed as armament instructor, Harwell, September 1939. Completed a specialist RAF armaments course. Posted out 6.2.40, recalled to New Zealand. Served in the Pacific, CO, 2 Squadron RNZAF (Ventura) 17.2.44. War Course at RAAF Staff College. Senior Air Staff Officer, 1 (Islands) Group RNZAF. Air Dept CO, RNZAF Hobsonville, 1947. CO, RNZAF Wigram, 1948. Awarded OBE 1950. Later air commodore. Died 20.1.96.

Hamilton, Aircraftman Ian Ferris McCarey, RAF 625294
Wireless Operator/Air Gunner
Posted in 13.11.39
Posted out some time before January 1940

Harkness, Pilot Officer Donald Joseph, RNZAF NZ37150/RAF 41694
Pilot
Posted in 27.11.39
A New Zealander in the RAF, he had initially joined the RNZAF 27.10.37 then been accepted for a short-service commission in the RAF and sailed to England in November 1938. Pilot's badge 23.9.39. Experience flying Whitleys. Posted to the New Zealand Squadron 27.11.39.
Flew 32 operations with 75 (NZ) Squadron (DFC citation says 34): two as 2nd pilot with the JN Collins crew, eight as 2nd pilot with the AAN Breckon crew, one with the WI Collett crew, and 21 with own crew. Awarded DFC 22.11.40.
Posted out 4.10.40 to 15 Operational Training Unit as an instructor, then to the Central Flying School, Hullavington, 23.8.41. Posted to 158 Squadron 18.2.42 and promoted to squadron leader. Flew seven operations with 158 Squadron.
Killed when his Wellington was shot down 30/31.5.42 by a German night fighter. Age 25, son of George Percy and Georgine McKay Harkness, of Midhurst, Taranaki, New Zealand; husband of Joan Harkness, of Esher, Surrey. Buried at Flushing (Vlissengen) Northern Cemetery, Holland.

Hewer, Corporal Albert, RAF 507903
Armourer
On attachment from RAF Abingdon
Ground role, did not fly operations

Hogg, Pilot Officer Richard John Kitchener, RAF 41702/131459
Pilot

Posted in mid-December 1939

A New Zealander in the RAF, obtaining his short-service commission in the RAF 28.12.38, with experience flying Whitleys.

Flew 35 operations with 75 (NZ) Squadron (including two DNC): 20 as 2nd pilot with the N Williams crew and 15 with his own crew.

Posted out 14.9.40. Flew General Bernard Freyberg VC from England to Malta, September 1940, in one of the first six Wellingtons to operate in Egypt. Flew operations with 70 Squadron (Wellington) stationed in Egypt, Greece and Libya and promoted to squadron leader. Awarded MiD 24.9.41. Awarded DFC (Immediate) 8.1.42. Third tour, flew operations with 115 Squadron. Had accumulated 58 operations by the time he returned to New Zealand in July 1942. On loan to the RNZAF. CO, 2 Squadron RNZAF, April–August 1943. Awarded DSO 14.7.44. RNZAF Reserve, May 1950. Territorial Air Force, November 1953 – December 1955.

Hopkins, Flying Officer John Price, RAF 37768
Pilot. Attached from 38 Squadron, Marham, May 1939.
Logged 0.50hrs flying with the New Zealand Squadron in May 1939
Awarded DFC 22.10.40. Squadron leader 6.6.44.

Hughes, Sergeant Robert Henry, RAF 550880
Observer
Posted in 13.11.39
Flew 35 operations with 75 (NZ) Squadron (including three DNC): 33 as observer with the AAN Breckon crew, one with the WI Collett crew, and one with the IR Gow crew. Awarded DFM 22.11.40.
Posted out September 1940

Hunter, Flight Lieutenant Charles Campbell, RNZAF NZ1023 (70011)
Pilot. Nominated pilot for the 1st Mobile Flight.
Foundation member, June 1939
Joined the NZAF in 1927 as one of the first ten cadet pilot trainees, under Chief Flying Instructor Maurice Buckley. Graduated and posted to 1 (AC) Squadron NZAF in 1930. Joined the RNZAF in October 1935, based at Wigram. Posted to the UK for RAF signals specialist training at Cranwell in 1937. Further training at the Royal Aeronautical Establishment, Farnborough. Served with an RAF maritime reconnaissance squadron, then posted to the New Zealand Squadron in June 1939. Course at Staff College, Andover, January 1940.
Posted out in February 1940, recalled to New Zealand. Staff Signals Officer, Air HQ, Wellington. Director of Signals, RNZAF, May 1942. While holding that post, in 1943 he studied developments in radar and signals in the UK and US. Commanding Officer, RNZAF Whenuapai, May 1945. Awarded OBE 1946. Director of Signals, Air Dept, Wellington. Director of Technical Services, RNZAF HQ, 1952. Air Member for Supply, Air Dept, 1957. Awarded CBE 1958. Died 16.9.89.

Hugill, Mr AT
Instrument Repairer
Civilian
Ground role, did not fly operations

Jenkins, Aircraftman Thomas Edward, RAF 614702
Flight Rigger
Foundation member, June 1939
Ground role, did not fly operations

Jones, Aircraftman Bernard Godfrey, RAF 616121
Flight Rigger

Foundation member, June 1939
Ground role, did not fly operations

Julian, Mr TN
Instrument Repairer
Civilian
Ground role, did not fly operations

Kay, Cyril Eyton 'Cyrus' OBE RNZAF NZ1011 (70004)/RAF 22223
Pilot. Nominated pilot and navigation officer for the 1st Mobile Flight.
Foundation member, June 1939. Squadron leader and navigation specialist.
Obtained a short-service commission with the RAF 14.6.26, specialised in navigation and meteorology. Elected a Fellow of the Royal Meteorological Society, 1928. Flew in the 1929 RAF Air Pageant set-piece displays at Hendon. In 1930, while still serving with the RAF, he co-piloted a Desoutter monoplane from Croydon to Darwin in an attempt to break the England-to-Australia record. Returned to New Zealand in 1932 and competed with two other New Zealanders in the 1934 MacRobertson centenary air race from England to Australia in the twin-engine de Havilland Dragon Rapide Tainui, then flew on to New Zealand, becoming the first NZ crew to cross the Tasman Sea by air. Joined the RNZAF 8.7.35 and became chief navigation instructor at 1 Flying Training School, Wigram, in March 1937. Flew to England in May 1939 to join the New Zealand Squadron.
Flew 22 operations with 75 (NZ) Squadron (including two DNC) with own crew and as flight commander of 'A' Flight. Awarded DFC 21.6.40. Presented with his DFC by the King at Buckingham Palace, 3.9.40.
Posted out 23.9.40 to Honington
Posted in 25.11.40. Wing commander and Officer Commanding, 75 (NZ) Squadron. Did not fly operations as OC.
Posted out 27.8.41. Returned to New Zealand and served as commanding officer at RNZAF training establishments at New Plymouth (1942–43), Ohakea (1943–44) and Wigram (1944–46). Attended the Imperial Defence College. Air Member for Supply, 1947. Acting Chief of the Air Staff. Awarded CBE 1.1.48. AOC, RNZAF HQ London, 1951. Air Member for Personnel, 1953. Air Vice-Marshal and Chief of the Air Staff RNZAF, 1956. Awarded CB 1.1.58. Retired 30.6.58. Died 29.4.93.

Kitson, Aircraftman Herbert James Hawkins 'Bert', RAF 625948
Wireless Operator/Air Gunner
Posted in 13.11.39
Flew 38 operations with 75 (NZ) Squadron (including two DNC): 35 as wireless operator with the J Adams crew, one with the CE Kay crew, and two with the WH Coleman crew. Awarded DFM 22.10.40.
Posted out September 1940
Killed in a training accident 27.9.41 at 20 Operational Training Unit; collided with another Wellington on landing. Age 20. Buried at Treorchy Cemetery.

Larney, Pilot Officer Geordie Keith 'Joe', RAF 33582
Pilot
Posted in 1.3.40
Learned to fly in New Zealand with the Wellington Aero Club, trained as a pilot with the RNZAF and obtained a short-service commission with the RAF in May 1939.
Flew 33 operations with 75 (NZ) Squadron: 12 as 2nd pilot with the J Adams crew and 21 with own crew. Awarded DFC 11.2.41.
Posted out 23.10.40. Seconded to a secret RAF unit working on airborne radar systems being developed to counter German night fighters. He married Pamela, an RAF meteorological officer, in September 1944. Retired from the RAF circa 1967 and lived in Little Stretton, England. Died 1.12.01.

Lucas, Corporal Albert Osmund, RAF 617003
Equipment Assistant
Foundation member, June 1939
Ground role, did not fly operations

Lucas, Flying Officer Frederick John 'Popeye', RNZAF NZ1056/RAF 39288
Pilot. Nominated pilot for the 1st Mobile Flight.
Foundation member, posted in 19.7.39
A New Zealander in the RAF, he obtained a short-service commission on 12.10.36 and flew Heyfords and Whitleys with 10 Squadron, Dishforth. Transferred to the RNZAF after posting to the New Zealand Squadron in July 1939. Listed as parachute officer when the squadron moved to Feltwell, 1.2.40.
Flew 37 operations with 75 (NZ) Squadron: two as 2nd pilot with the AAN Breckon crew, two with the JN Collins crew, and 33 with own crew. His party trick of swivelling his dentures in his mouth and resemblance to the cartoon character led to his nickname 'Popeye'; his flying feats and pranks were legendary in the squadron as was his aircraft, always painted with 'Popeye' nose art. Extended his first tour to 37 operations as determined to take part in a raid on Berlin. Awarded DFC 22.11.40. Awarded MiD 28.12.40.
Posted out 16.11.40 to 15 Operational Training Unit, Harwell. Posted to 1519 Beam Approach Training Flight.
Posted in for second tour 26.5.41, promoted to squadron leader and flight commander of 'A' Flight. Flew 16 operations as captain with own crew. Tragically, his wife Joan died in December 1941 and he decided to return home with their young daughter.

Posted out 10.1.42. Awarded a Bar to DFC 14.4.42. Returned to New Zealand, Officer Commanding, 1 General Reconnaissance Squadron (Hudson), Whenuapai, and, in 1943, helped form the RNZAF's first air transport unit, 40 (Transport) Squadron (Dakota) flying up to the Pacific Theatre. Married Lorie Flansburgh-Washbourne in April 1943. Returned to England after requesting a posting back to Bomber Command operations and is said to have been offered command of 75 (NZ) Squadron. Instead, he requested, and received, a posting as squadron leader and flight commander with 487 (NZ) Squadron, Hunsdon, flying Mosquitos. Returned to New Zealand, November 1945. Prominent in commercial aviation and farming in the Queenstown area after the war. Died 4.10.93, aged 78.

Mackay, Sergeant Donald, RAF 532942/44564
Observer
Posted in 13.11.39
Flew 32 operations with 75 (NZ) Squadron (including three DNC): 29 as observer with the N Williams crew, one with the FJ Lucas crew, one with the GK Larney crew, and one with the Neate crew.
Awarded DFM 13.9.40.
Posted out 2.5.41.
Posted to 7 Squadron, Oakington, flying Stirlings, crewed up again with his skipper from 75 (NZ) Squadron, F/L Neville Williams. Promoted to flying officer.
Lost with the Williams crew 11.5.41, came down near Cloppenburg during an attack on Berlin. Age 22, son of Mr and Mrs A. Mackay, Royal Oak Inn, Stamford Street, Altrincham. Buried at Becklingen War Cemetery, Germany.

Mair, Aircraftman Geoffrey Oswald Peter, RAF 619821
Flight Mechanic
Foundation member, June 1939
Ground role, did not fly operations

Mathews, Aircraftman HR, RAF 617706
Flight Mechanic
Foundation member, June 1939
Ground role, did not fly operations

McGlashan, Leading Aircraftman Donald Charles 'Don', RNZAF NZ37161 (70229)
Wireless Operator Mechanic/Wireless Electrical Mechanic. Nominated crew member for the 1st Mobile Flight.
Foundation member, July 1939
Enlisted in the RNZAF 20.10.37. One of the six wireless specialists, trained at the RNZAF's new Wireless School at Wigram, sent to England in January 1939 to train for the New Zealand Squadron ferry flights with Wellington squadrons in the RAF. Served with 99 Squadron. Posted to the New Zealand Squadron in July 1939.
Grounded in March 1940 due to the shortage of WOMs, did not fly operations.
Posted out May 1941. Awarded MiD 25.9.41. In November 1943, he attended the USN Fleet Radar School, Hawaii. Served in the Pacific as squadron leader and group radar officer, 1 (Islands) Group RNZAF HQ, Guadalcanal, under Maurice Buckley's command, and in Fiji, 1944–45. Second MiD awarded for service in the South Pacific, 10.7.45. Died 13.7.94.

Mead, Leading Aircraftman Thomas, RAF 43193
Armourer
On attachment from RAF Abingdon.
Ground role, did not fly operations.

Mees, Sergeant H, RAF
Fitter. Nominated crew member for the 1st Mobile Flight.
Foundation member, June 1939
Ground role
Posted out some time before January 1940

Meyer-Williams, Pilot Officer, RAF
Instructor pilot (attached from 38 Squadron, only at Marham, August 1939)

Mifflin, Aircraftman Joseph William Thomas, RAF 641371
Flight Mechanic
Posted in unknown date
Ground role, did not fly operations

Morrison, Flight Lieutenant Ian Gordon, RNZAF NZ1038 (70012)/RAF 37606
Pilot. Nominated pilot for the 2nd Mobile Flight.
Posted in 12.8.39
A New Zealander in the RAF, he obtained a short-service commission in the RAF in January 1936. Served with 44 Squadron flying Blenheims then took a special navigation course at Manston. Returned to New Zealand and transferred to the RNZAF in January 1939 but was posted back to England to join the New Zealand Squadron in mid-August 1939.
Posted out 3.2.40, recalled to New Zealand. Navigation instructor at the School of General Reconnaissance. Promoted to squadron leader and OC, 8 Squadron RNZAF (Vincent/Vildebeest). Senior Air Staff Officer, 1 (Islands) Group, Vanuatu. Wing commander and OC, 3 Squadron RNZAF (Ventura). Awarded OBE 1.1.46. Director of Organisation and Staff Duties, Air Dept, Wellington. Joint Services Staff College in England, then two years in the RAF. OC, RNZAF Ohakea. Member of the Air Board, 1954. Awarded CBE 1.1.57. Air vice-marshal and Chief of the Air Staff RNZAF, 1962. Awarded

CB 1.1.65. Retired in June 1966. Father of iconic New Zealand broadcaster Judy Bailey. Died 5.9.97, aged 83.

Mumby, Aircraftman Thomas Leonard, RAF 624569/49752
Wireless Operator/Air Gunner
Posted in February 1940
Flew 34 operations with 75 (NZ) Squadron: 32 as rear gunner then wireless operator with the AAN Breckon crew, one as wireless operator with the WI Collett crew, and one with the DV Gilmour crew. Awarded DFM 17.1.41.
Posted out September 1940. Re-trained as a pilot. To 144 Squadron, promoted to flight lieutenant, May 1944.
Lost with all crew 25.7.45 when his 194 Squadron Dakota crashed in Burma, circumstances unknown. Commemorated on the Singapore Memorial and on the Grimsby St. James Second World War Memorial.

Murphy, Aircraftman John Edgar, RAF 631909
Wireless Operator/Air Gunner
Posted in 13.11.39
Flew three operations with 75 (NZ) Squadron as front gunner with the WMC Williams crew.
Posted out May 1940. Wireless Intelligence Development Unit (WIDU).
Lost with all crew 8.11.40 when their WIDU Avro Anson hit a barrage-balloon cable in Birmingham. Age 19, son of George William and Edith Annie Murphy. Buried at West Bromwich Cemetery, United Kingdom.

Murphy, Aircraftman Patrick William 'Spud', RAF 616596
Flight Mechanic
Foundation member, June 1939
Ground role, did not fly operations

Nevill, Aircraftman William Eric, RAF 631165
Wireless Operator/Air Gunner
Posted in February 1940
Flew 22 operations with 75 (NZ) Squadron (including one DNC): one as rear gunner with the CE Kay crew, two as rear gunner with the N Williams crew, and 19 as wireless operator with the WH Coleman crew.
Lost on his 22nd operation with the Coleman crew near Amsterdam, returning from Kassel, 26.7.40. Age 23, son of William Thomas Nevill and Violet Gertrude Nevill, of Edmonton, Middlesex. Buried Amsterdam New Eastern Cemetery, Netherlands.

Parker, Corporal PS, RAF
Nominated crew member for the 1st Mobile Flight
Foundation member, June 1939
Ground role
Posted out some time before January 1940

Pearce, Leading Aircraftman Leslie Ernest Thomas, RAF 539947
Flight Mechanic. Nominated crew member for the 1st Mobile Flight.
Foundation member, June 1939
Ground role, did not fly operations

Pettit, Squadron Leader, RAF
Navigational instructor (at Marham, September 1939, possibly attached from 38 Squadron)

Pimbley, Leading Aircraftman George William, RAF 521600
Flight Mechanic
Foundation member, June 1939
Ground role, did not fly operations
Awarded MiD 11.3.41

Pomeroy, Corporal W, RAF
Fitter. Nominated crew member for the 1st Mobile Flight.
Foundation member, June 1939
Ground role
Posted out some time before 20.1.40

Rafferty, Aircraftman Edward, RAF 610072
Aircraft Hand
Posted in unknown date
Ground role, did not fly operations

Read, Aircraftman Frank, RAF 629401
Wireless Operator/Air Gunner
Posted in 13.11.39
No operations flown
Posted out November 1940

Read, Sergeant Thomas Richard 'Tutae' or 'Dick', RNZAF NZ34151 (70217)
Metal Rigger. Nominated crew member for the 1st Mobile Flight.
Foundation member, June 1939
Born in England but emigrated to Auckland, New Zealand. Served in the NZ Army/TF (Engineers). Enlisted in the RNZAF 4.5.34. Wigram, then Hobsonville in November 1937. Attached to the New Zealand-crewed Royal Navy cruiser HMS Achilles in 1937 employed servicing Supermarine Walrus aircraft, sailing to England in late 1938. Posted to the New Zealand Squadron in June 1939.
Ground role, did not fly operations
Awarded BEM 11.3.41
Posted out 25.2.41. Returned to New Zealand. Commissioned Engineering Officer 1.2.43 and served in the Pacific. Awarded MiD 1944. Died 24.4.60.

Renshaw, Leading Aircraftman John, RAF 538744
Flight Rigger. Nominated crew member for the 1st Mobile Flight.
Foundation member, June 1939
Ground role, did not fly operations
Awarded MiD 25.9.41

Rhodes, Aircraftman Alan, RAF 636739
Flight Mechanic
Posted in unknown date
Ground role, did not fly operations

Rider, Corporal William James, RAF 565772 (50752)
Wireless Radio Mechanic. Nominated crew member for the 1st Mobile Flight.
Foundation member, June 1939
Ground role, did not fly operations

Roberts, Flight Sergeant Edwin, RAF 343189
Fitter I. Engineering Officer/Office Administrator.

Foundation member, from May 1939
Ground role, did not fly operations
Awarded MBE 17.3.41

Rock, Aircraftman William Randolph, RAF 619261
Flight Mechanic
Posted in unknown date
Ground role, did not fly operations

Rose-Price, Flying Officer Arthur Thomas, RAF 39762
Pilot. Attached from 38 Squadron, Marham, May 1939.
Logged 0.50hrs flying with the New Zealand Squadron in May 1939
Posted from 38 Squadron to 10 Flying Training School on 29.9.39 as an instructor. Posted to 501 Squadron (Hurricane) at Kenley on 2.9.40, arrived in the morning, flew his first sortie and, on his second, that afternoon, was shot down and killed over Dungeness. Age 21, son of Samuel Percy Price and Anita Price (née Mackay), of Concepcion, Chile. Commemorated on the Runnymede Memorial.

Ross, Aircraftman Benjamin George, RAF 616595
Flight Mechanic
Posted in unknown date
Ground role, did not fly operations

Sach, Sergeant RAF
Instructor pilot (attached from 38 Squadron, only at Marham, late August–September 1939)
Appears to have logged only two flights with the New Zealand Squadron, one air test and a local practice, both on 31.8.39.

Shuttleworth, Sergeant Bernard, RAF 627701
Wireless Operator/Air Gunner
Posted in 13.11.39
Flew 12 operations with 75 (NZ) Squadron as front and rear gunner with the WH Coleman crew.
Posted out July 1940. To 99 Squadron, Newmarket, flying Wellingtons.
Lost with all crew 13.10.40, failed to return from an operation to Wilhelmshaven, lost without trace. Age 19, son of Alice Shuttleworth, of Bishop Auckland, Co. Durham. Commemorated on the Runnymede Memorial.

Smith, Aircraftman Richard 'Dick', RAF 615331
Flight Rigger
Foundation member, June 1939
Ground role, did not fly operations
Emigrated to New Zealand after the war

Smith, Aircraftman Harold, RAF 628540
Wireless Operator/Air Gunner
Posted in 13.11.39
Flew 29 operations with 75 (NZ) Squadron as wireless operator with the N Williams crew. Awarded DFM 13.9.40.
Posted out September 1940. Served with 17 Operational Training Unit.
Died 3.10.43 when his 17 OTU Wellington crashed and caught fire on landing at RAF Silverstone after an engine failed on a night navigation exercise. Six of eight crew killed. Age 23, son of Albert Verner Smith and Martha Smith of West Cornforth. Buried at Cornforth Holy Trinity Church, United Kingdom.

Steven, Sergeant William Douglas 'Bill', RNZAF NZ34153 (70210)
Fitter Aero Engines. Nominated crew member for the 1st Mobile Flight.
Foundation member, June 1939
From Auckland. Served with the RNVR 1930–33. Enlisted in the RNZAF 4.5.34. Attached to the New Zealand-crewed Royal Navy cruiser HMS Achilles in 1937, employed servicing Supermarine Walrus aircraft, sailing to England in late 1938. Posted to the New Zealand Squadron in June 1939.
Ground role, did not fly operations
Awarded MiD 25.9.41
Posted out January 1941. Returned to New Zealand, July 1941. Commissioned Engineering Officer, 1.2.43. Served in the Pacific as Engineering Officer, 30 Servicing Unit RNZAF (Avenger). Later squadron leader. Died 26.6.96.

Swetman, Corporal John Allan, RAF 565035
Fitter. Nominated crew member for the 1st Mobile Flight.
Foundation member, June 1939
Ground role
Posted out some time before January 1940

Taphouse, Aircraftman Henry Gerard, RAF 623843
Aircraft Hand
Posted in unknown date
Ground role, did not fly operations

Taylor, Leading Aircraftman Frank, RAF 521102
Flight Rigger
Foundation member, June 1939
Ground role, did not fly operations

Thomas, Aircraftman Eric William Wynn, RAF 546719
Armourer
On attachment from RAF Abingdon
Ground role, did not fly operations

Thorpe, Sergeant George, RAF 523426
Observer
Posted in 13.11.39
Flew 11 operations with 75 (NZ) Squadron as observer with the JN Collins crew.
Shot down on his 11th operation with the Collins crew near Tournai, Belgium, both pilots killed but the rest of the crew baled out and were immediately captured, 21/22.5.40. Wireless operator Brooks, rear gunner Hockey and Thorpe were the squadron's first POWs. PoW #5399. Safe UK, date unknown.

Turrell, Aircraftman Ernest, RAF 610368
Aircraft Hand
Posted in unknown date
Ground role, did not fly operations

Wallingford, Squadron Leader Sidney, RNZAF NZ1006 (70003)
Pilot. NZ Liaison Officer (NZLO) to the UK Air Ministry. Nominated as Commanding Officer, 3rd Mobile Flight.
Foundation member, June 1939
Made his way to England in 1916 to join the Army, serving in the Balkans. Joined the Royal Flying Corps in March 1918, flying in Egypt and Palestine. Returned to New Zealand, farmed and then had a stint in the Fiji Constabulary. NZAF 14.6.23. Rejoined the RAF 19.6.24, flying seaplanes and became

the two-time RAF rifle shooting champion. Returned to New Zealand in 1929 and served under Squadron Leader Len Isitt at Hobsonville, the new seaplane base near Auckland, as the first adjutant of the NZ Permanent Air Force. Flew the Air Force's first-ever active operational sortie, a 2hr 50min reconnaissance in a Gipsy Moth seaplane around the island of Upolu, Western Samoa, trying to spot Mau rebels in the bush. In 1931, he flew in medical and other supplies to Napier after the devastating earthquake. In 1935, he made the newspapers when he landed a Fairey IIIF seaplane beyond the breakers at Karekare Beach on Auckland's West Coast to rescue a woman who had been in the water for four hours, swept out to sea beyond the reach of surf-rescue teams. In 1936, he went back to the UK to attend RAF Staff College, Andover, then was appointed NZLO with the Air Ministry, London, a role which involved him in the purchase of the 30 Wellingtons for the RNZAF. Nominated as flight commander of the New Zealand Squadron's 3rd Mobile Flight. Assisted S/L Buckley with the initial setup of the squadron and accompanied him on two early Wellington collection flights from Weybridge, on 24 May and 14 June 1939. Served in his NZLO role in London for the first two years of the war.

Returned to New Zealand in 1941, appointed Air Member for Personnel at the Air Dept. In October 1942, promoted to group captain and appointed Senior RNZAF Officer co-operating with the American Forces in the Pacific, then Commander, 1 (Islands) Group. Awarded US Legion of Honour in 1943. Awarded CBE 1944. Appointed Air Officer Commanding Task Force Headquarters in 1945. Retired in 1954. Died 25.7.78, aged 80.

Watson, Flying Officer Samuel Miles Mackenzie, RAF 77026
Pilot
Posted in 27.11.39
A New Zealander in the RAF, he learned to fly while studying law at Cambridge University and was a member of the Wellington Territorial Squadron (Baffin) and Wellington Aero Club. Embarked for the UK 4.9.39 and took up his commission with the RAF in October 1939, 7 Squadron. Posted to the New Zealand Squadron 27.11.39. Listed as intelligence officer when the squadron moved to Feltwell, 1.2.40. Flew 15 operations with 75 (NZ) Squadron: five as 2nd pilot with the WMC Williams crew, ten with own crew. Awarded MiD 1.1.41.
Lost with all crew near Gelsenkirchen 20.7.40, probably shot down by fighters, age 27. Son of William & Louise Millicent Watson of Wellington, New Zealand. Buried at Reichswald Forest War Cemetery, Germany.

White, Aircraftman Jack, RAF 544659
Flight Rigger. Nominated crew member for the 1st Mobile Flight.
Foundation member, June 1939
Ground role, did not fly operations

White, Aircraftman Joseph Thomas, RNZAF NZ37178 (70235)
Wireless Operator Mechanic/Wireless Electrical Mechanic. Nominated crew member for the 1st Mobile Flight.
Foundation member, July 1939
From Christchurch. Enlisted in the RNZAF 20.10.37. One of the six wireless specialists, trained at the RNZAF's new wireless school at Wigram, who sailed to England on Rangitane in January 1939 to train for the New Zealand Squadron ferry flights with Wellington squadrons in the RAF. Served with 99 Squadron, Newmarket (Wellington). Posted to the New Zealand Squadron in July 1939.
Grounded in March 1940 due to the shortage of WOMs, did not fly operations.
Awarded MiD 11.3.41.
Posted out, 17.2.42. Returned to New Zealand, June 1942. Based at Ohakea. Later squadron leader.

White, Aircraftman Lewis Alan, RAF 626213
Wireless Operator/Air Gunner

Posted in 13.11.39

Flew 28 operations with 75 (NZ) Squadron: 26 as wireless operator, front gunner and rear gunner with the N Williams crew and two as wireless operator and rear gunner with the MR Braun crew. Awarded DFM 6.8.40.

Lost on his 28th operation, with the Braun crew, shot down 20.9.40 by coastal anti-aircraft batteries near Leffinge, Belgium. Age 20, son of Mr and Mrs HC White of Derby. Buried at Adegem Canadian War Cemetery, Belgium.

Williams, Leading Aircraftman Edwin Peter 'Ted', RNZAF NZ38235 (70231)
Wireless Operator. Nominated crew member for the 1st Mobile Flight.
Foundation member, July 1939

From Auckland, attended St. Stephen's Boys' School (Tipene). A keen amateur radio enthusiast, worked for Pan American Airways in Auckland before joining the RNZAF 4.5.38. One of the six wireless specialists, trained at the RNZAF's new Wireless School at Wigram, who sailed to England on Rangitane in January 1939 to train for the New Zealand Squadron ferry flights with Wellington squadrons in the RAF. Served with 99 Squadron, Newmarket (Wellington). Posted to the New Zealand Squadron in July 1939.

Flew 26 operations with 75 (NZ) Squadron: eight as wireless operator with the AAN Breckon crew (including the epic 14-hour Narvik reconnaissance flight of 12.4.40), one as wireless operator with the CE Kay crew, and 17 as wireless operator with the WI Collett crew. Injured in a bad crash 3.8.40 when his Wellington made a wheels-up crash landing with a dead engine at Barton Mills. On return from an attack on Gelsenkirchen, they had been diverted from Feltwell to Mildenhall but ran into a fog bank and flew into the ground, catching fire. The pilot, S/L WI Collett, was injured seriously and died later that day. Awarded DFM 6.8.40. Newly married, Williams used his sick leave to go on his honeymoon! Commissioned as pilot officer, August 1941.

Thought to have stayed on with 75 (NZ) Squadron for a second tour, promoted to flying officer and squadron signals leader. Mentioned in December 1941 newspaper reports for leading a haka at Feltwell in honour of the new governor-general, Sir Cyril Newall.

Posted out 9.9.42. Signals School. Returned to New Zealand. Staff Officer Signals, 1 (Islands) Group in the Pacific, from October 1944 to July 1945. Flew as navigator on RNZAF Mosquito ferry flights 1946–47. Later squadron leader, 75 Squadron RNZAF. Died 29.9.92.

Williams, Flying Officer Neville, RNZAF NZ1068/RAF 40039
Pilot. Nominated Pilot for the 1st Mobile Flight.
Foundation member, 24 July 1939

From Frankton Junction, he learned to fly at the Western Federated Flying Club, gaining his A License in 1936 and obtained a short-service commission in the RAF 31.5.37, where he had experience flying Harrows. Transferred to the RNZAF after posting to the New Zealand Squadron on 24.7.39. Listed as armament officer when the squadron moved to Feltwell, 1.2.40.

Flew 33 operations with 75 (NZ) Squadron (including two DNC) with own crew. Awarded DFC (Immediate) 6.8.40. Presented with DFC by the King at Buckingham Palace, 3.9.40.

Posted out 8.9.40 to 11 Operational Training Unit, Bassingbourn, as an instructor. Posted to 7 Squadron, Oakington, one of the first squadrons to operate Stirlings. Teamed up with his navigator from 75 (NZ) Squadron, F/O Donald Mackay DFM. Promoted to flight lieutenant. Awarded MiD 17.3.41.

Lost with all of his crew on 11.5.41, shot down by a night fighter near Cloppenburg during an attack on Berlin. Age 26, son of Mrs AJ Meyer, Auckland. Buried at Becklingen War Cemetery, Soltau, Niedersachsen, Germany.

Williams, Flying Officer Wilfred Maurice Chalk 'Bill', RNZAF NZ1057
Pilot. Nominated Pilot for the 1st Mobile Flight.

Foundation member, 17 July 1939

A New Zealander in the RAF, from Wanganui, he travelled to England in 1935 and in March 1936 obtained a short-service commission in the RAF. Served with 9 Squadron flying Heyfords and Wellingtons. Transferred to the RNZAF after posting to the New Zealand Squadron, 17.7.39.

Flew 32 operations with 75 (NZ) Squadron (including two DNC) with his own crew. Awarded DFC 22.11.40.

Posted out 29.8.40. Posted to 311 (Czechoslovakian) Squadron, Beale, as a pilot instructor and Training Flight CO. Posted to 218 Squadron (Wellington) 7.10.41. Promoted to squadron leader 11.11.41. Awarded MiD 1.1.42. Posted to 1521 Beam Approach Training Flight 23.1.42. Returned to New Zealand in March 1942. Commanding Officer, 1 Operational Training Unit, RNZAF Ohakea (Hudson). Died 15.7.43 when his Lockheed Hudson crashed on taking off from Ohakea on a night flying exercise, catching fire and killing all three on board. Age 30, son of The Revd. Canon Wilfred Gaster Williams and Madeline Williams, of Wanganui; husband of Kathleen Penelope Williams, of Fielding. Buried at Aramoho Cemetery, Wanganui, New Zealand.

Yates, Aircraftman Arthur Holmes, RAF 611875
Aircraft Hand
Posted in unknown date
Ground role, did not fly operations

~ ~ ~ ~ ~ ~ ~ ~

Sources:

Formation of No 75 (NZ) Squadron from the New Zealand Flight, letter from M.W. Buckley, dated 29.5.40.

Monthly Flying Times, May – August 1939, New Zealand Squadron, M.W. Buckley, Archives New Zealand, M.W. Buckley collection.

New Zealand Squadron Flight Authorisation Book, May 1939 – June 1940, Air Force Museum of New Zealand.

New Zealand Squadron Nominal Rolls dated 8.1.40 and 20.1.40, M.W. Buckley collection, Archives New Zealand.

Schedule of Officers and Airmen Crews, ... 1st Mobile Flight, S/L Sid Wallingford, dated 15.8.39, M.W. Buckley collection, Archives New Zealand.

Nominal Roll, 75nzsquadron.com, at https://75nzsquadron.wordpress.com/nr-index-access-page/.

75 (NZ) Squadron Personnel Records, compiled by Group Captain C.M. Hanson OBE RNZAF (Rtd), 75 Squadron RAF-RNZAF Association.

Appendix 2

List of 1st Mobile Flight personnel

Officers and airmen scheduled to leave United Kingdom for New Zealand in six RNZAF Wellington Mark IA aircraft (NZ306–311) on 1.10.39:

F/O John 'Jack' Adams, RNZAF NZ1027
2nd Pilot NZ308

AC1 Ronald Alexander John Anderson, RNZAF NZ36139
Wireless Operator NZ307

F/O Aubrey Arthur Ninnis 'Breck' Breckon, RNZAF NZ1025, 70016
Captain NZ307, callsign ZM-ZAC

S/L Maurice William 'Buck' Buckley, RNZAF NZ1005
Commanding Officer NZ Squadron and Commanding Officer 1st Mobile Flight
Captain NZ306, callsign ZM-ZAB

Sgt Rupert Percy Frank Colbourn, RAF 564590
Instrument Maker NZ309

P/O William Harcourt 'Bill' Coleman, RNZAF NZ2526, 39781
2nd Pilot NZ310

F/O John Noel Collins, RNZAF NZ2513
Captain NZ309, callsign ZM-ZAE

Cpl A Colville, RAF
Fitter NZ309

LAC Albert Eric Emery, RAF 518344
Wireless Radio Mechanic/Flight Mechanic NZ310

P/O Trevor Owen Freeman, RNZAF NZ1026
2nd Pilot NZ307

Cpl Alexander Duf Gordon, RAF 564496
Wireless and Electrical Mechanic NZ308

F/O Arthur Beale Greenaway, RNZAF NZ1034
Captain NZ310, callsign ZM-ZAF

F/L Charles Campbell Hunter, RNZAF NZ1023
Captain NZ308, callsign ZM-ZAD

S/L Cyril Eyton 'Cyrus' Kay, RNZAF NZ1011, 22223
Navigational Officer 1st Mobile Flight
2nd Pilot NZ306

F/O Frederick John 'Popeye' Lucas, RNZAF NZ1056
2nd Pilot NZ311

AC1 Donald Charles 'Don' McGlashan, RNZAF NZ37161
Wireless Operator/Wireless and Electrical Mechanic NZ309

Sgt H Mees, RAF
Fitter NZ311

Cpl PS Parker, RAF
(trade not known) NZ307

AC1 Leslie Ernest Thomas Pearce, RAF 539947
Flight Mechanic NZ311

Cpl W Pomeroy, RAF
Fitter NZ310

Cpl Thomas Richard Read, RNZAF, NZ34151
Metal Rigger/Airframe Fitter NZ306

AC1 John Renshaw, RAF 538744
Flight Rigger NZ307

Cpl W J Rider, RAF 565772
Wireless Radio Mechanic NZ306

Cpl William Douglas 'Bill' Steven, RNZAF NZ34153
Fitter Aero Engines NZ306

Cpl John Allan Swetman, RAF 565035
Fitter NZ308

AC1 Jack White, RAF 544659
Flight Rigger NZ308

AC1 Joseph Thomas 'Joe' White, RNZAF NZ37178, 70235
Wireless Operator/Wireless and Electrical Mechanic NZ311

LAC Edwin Peter 'Ted' Williams, RNZAF, NZ38235
Wireless Operator NZ310

P/O Neville Williams, RNZAF NZ1068
2nd Pilot NZ309

P/O Wilfred Maurice Chalk 'Bill' Williams, RNZAF NZ1057
Captain NZ311, callsign ZM-ZAG

Appendix 3

List of 2nd–4th Mobile Flights personnel

While none of the remaining four mobile flights were formed up, by the time the RNZAF Wellington ferry flight plan was cancelled, several individuals had been nominated to join the New Zealand Squadron and two had already commenced training at Marham.

2nd Mobile Flight

Expected to commence training on 1.10.39 and leave the UK on 1.12.39.

S/L Ronald Joseph 'Nugget' Cohen RNZAF NZ1015
Pilot and Commanding Officer
Posted to Marham mid-August 1939 and commenced training
Under the original plan, Cohen would have taken over command of the New Zealand Squadron when Buckley left with the 1st Mobile Flight on 1.10.39, and then left for New Zealand with the 2nd Mobile Flight on 1.12.39.
Posted out January 1940, recalled to New Zealand. See Appendix 1.

F/O Ian Gordon Morrison RNZAF NZ1038 / RAF 37606
Pilot
Posted to Marham 12.8.39 and commenced training
Posted out 3.2.40, recalled to New Zealand. See Appendix 1.

F/O Charles Hampton 'Charlie' Clark RAF 39272
Pilot and navigation specialist
Not posted to Marham
A New Zealander serving in the RAF, he had travelled to England in 1936 to join up, commissioned as a pilot officer in September 1937. Played rugby for the RAF. Led a flight of bombers out to Iraq in August 1938. By 1939, he was flying Hudsons with 233 Squadron, based at Leuchars in Scotland. Killed on 10.10.39 returning from patrol at low level in poor visibility and a low cloud base, crashed into high ground and caught fire at Drums, 1.5 miles south of Freuchie, Fife, Scotland. Fire broke out immediately on impact and the wreckage was distributed over a wide area. All four crew were killed. Age 27, son of John and Nora Clark, Wellington, New Zealand. Buried at Leuchars Cemetery.

LAC Graham Hunter French RNZAF NZ38159
Wireless Operator
From Rotorua. Trained as a wireless operator at Wigram. Sailed from Wellington on *Rangitiki* on 29.7.39, arriving in England exactly a month later. Attached to the RAF and posted to 99 Squadron, Mildenhall (Wellington), 1.9.39. Following the outbreak of war, the Wellington ferry flights were cancelled, so he was not posted to the New Zealand Squadron. Posted to 485 (NZ) Squadron, operating Spitfires in March 1941. Returned to New Zealand. 25 Squadron RNZAF, Dauntless air gunner, 1943. Promoted to flying officer 1.5.44. Whenuapai, 1945. Post-war Radio Officer, Tasman Empire Airways Limited. Died 29.8.87.

LAC Francis Maitland Bissett Frank George RNZAF NZ37231 (70236)
Wireless Electrical Mechanic
From Auckland. Joined the RNZAF 1.11.37. Trained as a WEM in the first RNZAF wireless course at Wigram. Played rugby for Canterbury. Sailed from Wellington on *Rangitiki* on 29.7.39, arriving in England a month later. 99 Squadron, Mildenhall (Wellington), 1.9.39. Followed French to 485 (NZ)

Squadron in March 1941. Returned to New Zealand in November 1941, married 6.12.41. Commissioned as signals officer, March 1942. 7 Squadron, Waipapakauri. Northern Group HQ. 5 Servicing Unit. Base Depot, Espiritu Santo. OC, Signals Repair Section, 1 Repair Depot, Hamilton and Ohakea. Staff Officer Signals, Air Dept, 1947. Station Signals Officer, Whenuapai, 1951. Awarded MBE in 1953. Later wing commander. Two of his brothers served in the RNZAF during the war. Died 22.6.80.

LAC Trevor James Goodhue RNZAF NZ38113
Wireless Operator

From Taumarere, Bay of Islands. Worked in a radio factory in Auckland. Joined the RNZAF, trained as a wireless operator at Wigram. Sailed from Wellington on *Rangitiki* on 29.7.39, disembarking in England exactly a month later. Attached to the RAF and posted to 99 Squadron at Mildenhall, 1.9.39. The outbreak of war saw the end of the Wellington ferry flight plan, so not posted to the New Zealand Squadron. Met the King at New Zealand House on 20 October that year.
Posted to 75 (NZ) Squadron 29.7.40.
Flew 22 operations with 75 (NZ) Squadron (including one DNC): 15 as wireless operator with the RM Curtis crew and seven with the AP Jones crew.
Posted out 29.11.40. Returned to New Zealand, August 1941. Groomsman at Frank George's wedding, December 1941. Later flying officer, 30 Squadron and Servicing Unit, Gisborne. Settled in Gisborne after the war, farming at Patutahi. Died 30.7.93, aged 79.

LAC Norman Cook Murray RNZAF
Wireless Electrical Mechanic

From Wanganui. Trained as a WEM at Wigram. Sailed from Wellington on *Rangitiki* on 29.7.39. Attached to the RAF and posted to 99 Squadron, Mildenhall (Wellington), 1.9.39. Eventually joined French and George at 485 (NZ) Squadron, operating Spitfires, in March 1941. Returned to New Zealand by 1943 as a flying officer. Farmed in Waihi after the war, then insurance inspector, Wellington. Died 21.4.67, aged 51.

LAC George Oscar Perrott RNZAF NZ37168
Wireless Electrical Mechanic

From Christchurch. Enlisted in the RNZAF 20.10.37. Trained as a WEM in the first RNZAF wireless course at Wigram. Sailed from Wellington on *Rangitiki* on 29.7.39. 99 Squadron 1.9.39. Returned to New Zealand in November 1941, having not served with the New Zealand Squadron. Best man at Frank George's wedding, December 1941. Promoted to pilot officer and signals officer 1.6.42. Signals Officer, RNZAF Whenuapai. Posted to 14 Squadron. Promoted to flying officer 1.5.43. Chief Signals Officer, RNZAF Fighter Wing, Guadalcanal. Awarded MiD 22.3.46. Died 21.7.89.

LAC Thomas Gray Smith RNZAF NZ38215 (70239)
Wireless Electrical Mechanic

Born 4.12.10. From New Plymouth. Trained as a WEM at Wigram. Sailed from Wellington on *Rangitiki* on 29.7.39, arriving in England exactly a month later. Attached to the RAF and posted to 99 Squadron, 31.8.39. Not posted to the New Zealand Squadron following the outbreak of war as the ferry flights to New Zealand were cancelled. Wounded in an air raid on 27.10.40 and admitted to Newmarket Hospital with back injuries. Posted to 485 (NZ) Squadron (Spitfire), 31.3.41 (some documentation suggests he was then posted to 75 (NZ) Squadron). Returned to New Zealand, circa 1942. Flying officer 10.3.43. Later squadron leader. Retired 1961. Died 6.6.81, aged 70.

3rd Mobile Flight

Expected to commence training on 1.12.39 and leave the UK in February 1940.

S/L Sidney Wallingford, RNZAF NZ1006
Pilot and Commanding Officer. Also NZSLO London.

Not posted to Marham

Assisted Buckley with Wellington deliveries in May but no training undertaken at Marham. Under the original plan, Wallingford would have taken command of the New Zealand Squadron when S/L Cohen left with the 2nd Mobile Flight on 1.12.39, and then left for New Zealand with the 3rd Mobile Flight in July 1940. See Appendix 1.

4th Mobile Flight

Expected to commence training on 1.7.40 and leave the UK around September or October 1940.

Squadron Leader James Lloyd 'Fin' Findlay MC, RNZAF NZ1004
Pilot and Commanding Officer

Not posted to Marham

Under the original plan, Findlay would have assumed command of the New Zealand Squadron when S/L Wallingford left with the 3rd Mobile Flight in July 1940, and then left for New Zealand with the 4th Mobile Flight in Sept–Oct 1940.

Findlay served in the British Army (earning a Military Cross) and the Royal Flying Corps in the First World War. In June 1923, he became one of the founding officers of the New Zealand Permanent Air Force and commanded Wigram aerodrome from 1926 to 1938. Attached to the RAF on exchange in January 1938 and at the outbreak of war he was OC, 48 Squadron, Bicester, operating Avro Ansons. Station Commander, RAF Hooton Park then recalled to New Zealand. Deputy Chief of the Air Staff, Air Dept. AOC Central Group, September 1942. New Zealand Head of the Joint Staff Mission and RNZAF Representative to Combined Chiefs of Staff, Washington, D.C., USA. Awarded CBE 1.1.44. Awarded US Legion of Merit 7.11.46. New Zealand Air Attaché in Washington, D.C. Retired in 1954. Died 17.3.83, Richmond, Surrey, England, aged 87.

5th Mobile Flight

No details of personnel available.

Mark I, Type 403 (RNZAF variant), Contract No. 781439/38
RAF serial number L4313, allocated to RNZAF. Cancelled. Replaced by L4340, allocated to RNZAF as NZ302.
Dual control set
Manufactured April–May 1939, Vickers-Armstrongs, Weybridge
Test flown at Weybridge by 'Mutt' Summers, 20.5.39, 12:25 hrs, 15 mins, with Bob Rampling, Vickers Flight Engineer
Test flown at Weybridge by 'Mutt' Summers, 22.5.39, 13:25 hrs, with Mr Green, VID
Delivered to NZ Squadron, Marham, 24.5.39
Coded 'C'. Re-coded 'B' in early October 1939.
Re-serialled **L4340** on 14.11.39 and added to Contract No. 781439/38. RAF Movement Card issued. Not flown after replacement Mark IAs received on 25.1.40, except for a short 15-min hop across to Methwold on 21.4.40. Possibly re-coded 'M' (from photograph at Silloth).
Despatched to Silloth by air 3.5.40
To 22 MU, Silloth, 3.5.40. To 15 Operational Training Unit, Harwell 18.11.41. To 27 OTU 9.1.42. Conversion to Mark XV passenger transport configuration at Vickers Weybridge 12.6.42. To 45 MU 5.9.42. To 24 Squadron, Ferry Command, Hendon, 1.12.42. Coded NQ-A, named *Duke of Rutland*. Repairs Vickers Weybridge 4.1.43. R&M 26 MU 7.2.44. R&M 8 MU 9.8.44. Cat E damage 19.11.44. Struck off charge 19.11.44

NZ303

Mark I, Type 403 (RNZAF variant), Contract No. 781439/38
RAF serial number L4314, allocated to RNZAF. Cancelled. Replaced by L4350, allocated to RNZAF as NZ303.
Dual control set
Manufactured May 1939, Vickers-Armstrongs, Weybridge
Test flown at Weybridge by 'Mutt' Summers, 8–10.6.39
Delivered to NZ Squadron, Marham, 14.6.39
Coded 'D'. Re-coded 'C' in early October 1939
Re-serialled **L4350** on 14.11.39 and added to Contract No. 781439/38. RAF Movement Card issued. Taken on charge, RAF Stradishall, 16.1.40. Not often flown after replacement Mark IAs were received on 25.1.40. 40 min flight on 1.3.40 Collins, Feltwell-Stradishall and return.
Flown out of Feltwell to Silloth 6.3.40
To 22 MU, Silloth, 6.3.40. To 12 OTU 13.3.42. ROS, Vickers Weybridge, 10.5.42. To 14 OTU 4.12.42. Repairs AGT RIW 21.8.43. R&M 18 MU 6.3.44.
Struck off charge 21.3.46. Scrapped 31.9.46.

NZ304

Mark I, Type 403 (RNZAF variant), Contract No. 781439/38
RAF serial number L4315, allocated to RNZAF. Cancelled. Replaced by L4355, allocated to RNZAF as NZ304.
Dual control set
Manufactured May 1939, Vickers-Armstrongs, Weybridge
Test flown at Weybridge by 'Mutt' Summers 13.6.39
Delivered to NZ Squadron, Marham, 20.6.39
Coded 'E'. Re-coded 'D' in early October 1939.
Re-serialled **L4355** on 14.11.39 and added to Contract No. 781439/38. RAF Movement Card issued. Taken on charge, RAF Stradishall, 16.1.40. Not flown for three months after replacement Mark IAs were received on 25.1.40, but then re-activated for training use. After an air test on 16.4.40, Buckley took it on a 25-minute local flight to check flaps and throttle-rod issues. Flown by Lucas on 21.4.40 to

Appendix 4

The NZ Wellingtons

The first batch of six aircraft manufactured for the RNZAF were Mark Is to be used to train the fe flight crews selected to fly 30 Wellington bombers back to New Zealand. They were to remain at Marh while the first four flights trained and flew out to New Zealand and then used as the aircraft for the f and final flight.

Manufactured with RNZAF serial numbers.

NZ300

Mark I, Type 403 (RNZAF variant), Contract No. 781439/38
RAF serial number L4311, allocated to RNZAF as NZ300
Dual control set
Manufactured April 1939, Vickers-Armstrongs, Weybridge
First test flight ca. mid-April
Flown from Weybridge 25.4.40 to unknown airfield for official delivery/handover to NZ Governme representatives 27.4.40.
Test flown at Weybridge by 'Mutt' Summers, 19.5.39, 16:20 hrs, 20 mins, with Bob Handasyde, Vic Flight Test Observer
Test flown at Weybridge by 'Mutt' Summers, 10.7.39 and 13.7.39
Fuel jettison test flights at Weybridge by Maurice Hare, 25.7.39, 24.8.39, 25.8.39
Never delivered to New Zealand Squadron, Marham
To 5 Maintenance Unit, RAF Kemble, 11.39, 'reserve aircraft'
Re-serialled **L4311** 11.11.39 and added to Contract No. 781439/38. RAF Movement Card issued.
To 4 MU 24.2.40. To the Central Gunnery School, Warmwell, 29.5.40. R&M 48 MU 2.5.41. R&M 3 MU 11.7.41. R&M 48 MU 3.10.41. To 1 BAS as Instructional Airframe 3037M, Watchfield, 1941.
Struck off charge 8.4.42. Reduced to scrap 25.2.44.

NZ301

Mark I, Type 403 (RNZAF variant), Contract No. 781439/38
RAF serial number L4312, allocated to RNZAF. Cancelled. Replaced by L4330, allocated to RNZAF NZ301.
Dual control set
Manufactured April–May 1939, Vickers-Armstrongs, Weybridge
Delivered to NZ Squadron, Marham, 24.5.39
Coded 'B'. Re-coded 'A' in early October 1939.
Re-serialled **L4330** on 14.11.39 and added to Contract No. 781439/38. RAF Movement Card issue
Taken on charge, RAF Stradishall, 16.1.40. Not often flown after replacement Mark IAs were receiv on 25.1.40. To Feltwell 1.3.40.
Flown out of Feltwell to Silloth 6.3.40.
To 22 MU, Silloth 6.3.40. To 30 MU 13.2.41. To 3 BAT Flt, Mildenhall, 14.7.41. To 4 School of Technical Training, St.Athan, 1.10.41, where used as an instructional airframe.
Struck off charge 1.2.44

NZ302

Newmarket, Stradishall and back (1 hour). Then, on 22.4.40, re-coded 'Z', Collins flew a three-hour cross-country to Northampton, Somerston, Northampton and return. Freeman flew across to Methwold on 26.4.40.

Transferred to 11 OTU, Bassingbourn, delivered by air 17.6.40. R&M Vickers Brooklands SAS 15.10.40. Damaged Cat AC 31.2.41. FA Cat E damage, stalled and crashed near Steeple Morden during night circuit practice, all three crew killed, a/c burnt out, 8.7.41.

Struck off charge 15.7.41. Total Flying Hours 321.50.

NZ305

Mark I, Type 403 (RNZAF variant), Contract No. 781439/38
RAF serial number L4316, allocated to RNZAF. Cancelled. Replaced by L4360, allocated to RNZAF as NZ305.
Manufactured June 1939, Vickers-Armstrongs, Weybridge
Delivered to NZ Squadron, Marham, 29.6.39
Coded 'F'. Re-coded 'E' in early October 1939.
Re-serialled **L4360** on 14.11.39 and added to Contract No. 781439/38. RAF Movement Card issued.
Taken on charge, RAF Stradishall, 16.1.40. Not flown after replacement Mark IAs were received on 25.1.40.
Flown out of Feltwell to Silloth 6.3.40 (incorrectly entered as 'L4340' in the Flight Authorisation Book).
To 22 MU, Silloth, 6.3.40. To 15 OTU, Harwell, 5.6.40. To 20 OTU, Lossiemouth, 6.6.40. R&M Vickers Brooklands 13.8.40. FA Cat AC damage 3.5.41. FA Cat E damaged beyond repair 29.6.41, overshot on landing, u/c collapsed.
Struck off charge 17.7.41. Total Flying Hours 522.15.

~ ~ ~ ~ ~ ~ ~ ~

The second batch of six aircraft manufactured were Mark IAs, intended as the first six aircraft to be flown back to New Zealand, making up the '1st Mobile Flight', which was due to depart for New Zealand on 1 October 1939.

Six consecutive RAF serial numbers were allocated to the RNZAF, N2874–2879. These aircraft were apparently all built by the time the RNZAF order was cancelled on 4 September, manufactured with RNZAF serial numbers, NZ306–311.

None were delivered to the New Zealand Squadron, however five were delivered to Marham, to fly with Nos. 115 and 38 Squadrons.

NZ306

Mark IA, Type 412 (RNZAF variant), Contract No. 781439/38
RAF serial number N2874, allocated to RNZAF as NZ306
Manufactured July–August 1939, Vickers-Armstrongs, Weybridge
Fitted with LRASV radar set
RNZAF order cancelled and re-directed to RAF 4.9.39
Re-serialled **N2874** on 10.9.39. RAF Movement Card issued.
To A&AEE 1.12.39. R&M 48 MU 25.5.40. To IAAS 8.11.40. Repairs Cat AC damage 7.12.41. To Central Gunnery School 3.5.43. Cat E1 damage (written off) 16.8.43.
Struck off charge 16.8.43 and converted to instructional airframe 22.10.43.

NZ307

Mark IA, Type 412 (RNZAF variant), Contract No. 781439/38
RAF serial number N2875, allocated to RNZAF as NZ307
Manufactured July–August 1939, Vickers-Armstrongs, Weybridge
RNZAF order cancelled and re-directed to RAF 4.9.39
Re-serialled **N2875** on 10.9.39. RAF Movement Card issued.
To 115 Squadron, Marham, 17.9.39. Cat I damage 31.5.40. Repairs 33 MU 1.6.40. To 305 Squadron 29.12.40. To 11 OTU 13.6.41. ROS Vickers 9.11.41. Cat AC damage ROS 9.2.42. To 16 OTU 15.9.42. To 26 OTU 11.10.42. Repairs Cat AC damage 9.12.42. To CGS, Catfoss, 21.1.43. R&M 23 MU 12.6.43. Repairs Cat B damage 11.11.43. R&M 18 MU 11.8.44.
Struck off charge 8.1.46
At some point this aircraft was converted to a Mark XV in passenger transport configuration.

NZ308

Mark IA, Type 412 (RNZAF variant), Contract No. 781439/38
RAF serial number N2876, allocated to RNZAF as NZ308
Manufactured July–August 1939, Vickers-Armstrongs, Weybridge
RNZAF order cancelled and re-directed to RAF 4.9.39
Re-serialled **N2876** on 10.9.39. RAF Movement Card issued.
To 115 Squadron Marham 17.9.39. To 11 OTU 22.3.40. FA Cat AC 23.7.41. ROS Vickers Weybridge 18.9.42. To CGS 5.2.43. FA Cat E crashed Terrington Marsh after double engine failure on a cine-gun exercise 22.3.43.
Struck off charge 12.4.43

NZ309

Mark IA, Type 412 (RNZAF variant), Contract No. 781439/38
RAF serial number N2877, allocated to RNZAF as NZ309
Manufactured August 1939, Vickers-Armstrongs, Weybridge
RNZAF order cancelled and re-directed to RAF 4.9.39
Re-serialled **N2877** on 10.9.39. RAF Movement Card issued.
To 115 Squadron, Marham, 17.9.39. *To No 75 (NZ) Squadron, Feltwell, 10.3.40.* To 15 OTU 18.4.40. FA Cat AC, 10.7.41. ROS Vickers, 2.11.41. ROS MR, 8.2.42. FA Cat AC Vickers Weybridge, 15.6.42. To 15 OTU 27.6.42. To 16 OTU 10.9.42. FA Cat AC 21.9.42. ROS Vickers Weybridge 24.7.42. To 26 OTU 27.10.42. To CGS 21.1.43. ROS Vickers Weybridge 18.2.43. Repairs damage Cat B Vickers Weybridge 2.8.43. To 18 MU 19.4.44. To 303 Flying Training Unit 11.5.44. To 1 Overseas Aircraft Despatch Unit 16.5.44. Despatched to West Africa Command 17.5.44.
Struck off charge 1.1.47
At some point this aircraft was converted to a Mark XV.

NZ310

Mark IA, Type 412 (RNZAF variant), Contract No. 781439/38
RAF serial number N2878, allocated to RNZAF as NZ310
Manufactured August 1939, Vickers-Armstrongs, Weybridge
RNZAF order cancelled and re-directed to RAF 4.9.39
Re-serialled **N2878** on 15.9.39. RAF Movement Card issued.
To 115 Squadron, Marham, 17.9.39. To 38 Squadron, Marham, 30.11.39. R&M Vickers 4 MU 11.3.40. R&M 24 MU 2.4.40. FA 27.5.40. R&M Vickers 4 MU 24.6.40. R&M 24 MU 26.7.40. To 12 OTU 19.11.40. To Royal Aircraft Establishment 20.6.41. RAAA 20.2.42. R&M 44 MU 23.3.42. R&M 18 M 10.10.43. Cat E1 28.3.44.

NZ311

Mark IA, Type 412 (RNZAF variant), Contract No. 781439/38
RAF serial number N2879, allocated to RNZAF as NZ311
Manufactured August 1939, Vickers-Armstrongs, Weybridge
RNZAF order cancelled and re-directed to RAF 4.9.39.
Re-serialled **N2879** on 10.9.39. RAF Movement Card issued.

To 5 MU 16.9.39 (Reserves for Bomber Command). To 38 Squadron, Marham, 23.9.39. LAC J Copley, the rear gunner in Wellington N2879 'Z-Zebra' claimed an enemy fighter destroyed, 38 Squadron's first of the war, 3.12.39. R&M 24 MU 21.4.40. R&M 22 MU 14.5.40. R&M 5 MU 16.9.40. ROS Vickers 12.10.41. R&M 5 MU 15.11.41. To FTU 10.12.41. R&M 8 MU 19.5.42. Cat E 19.11.44.
Struck off charge 19.11.44

~ ~ ~ ~ ~ ~ ~ ~

The third batch of six aircraft manufactured were Mark IAs, intended for the '2nd Mobile Flight', which was due to depart for New Zealand in January 1940.

Six consecutive RAF serial numbers were allocated to the RNZAF, N2937–2942. These aircraft were not completed when the RNZAF order was cancelled on 4 September 1939 and were allocated RAF serial numbers, so never had 'NZ' serial numbers.

None were delivered to the New Zealand Squadron.

Incredibly, three of these aircraft were lost on the same operation on 18 December 1939.

N2937 (ordered as NZ312)

Mark IA, Type 412 (RNZAF variant), Contract No. 781439/38
RAF serial number N2937, allocated to RNZAF
Dual control set
Manufactured September–October 1939, Vickers-Armstrongs, Weybridge
RNZAF order cancelled and re-directed to RAF 4.9.39
To 37 Squadron, Feltwell, 21.10.39 (to replace Mark Is). FA 3.8.40. *To No. 75 (NZ) Squadron, Feltwell, 6.11.40.* To 18 (Gold Coast) Squadron, Oakington, 13.11.40. R&M 46 MU 10.4.41. R&M Vickers SAS 24.4.41.
Struck off charge 1.5.41. Total Flying Hours 181.45.

N2938 (ordered as NZ313)

Mark IA, Type 412 (RNZAF variant), Contract No. 781439/38
RAF serial number N2938, allocated to RNZAF
Manufactured September-October 1939, Vickers-Armstrongs, Weybridge
RNZAF order cancelled and re-directed to RAF 4.9.39
To 37 Squadron, Feltwell, 23.10.39 (to replace Mark Is). R&M 45 MU 5.5.40. To 57 Squadron, Feltwell, 23.11.40. To 311 (Czech) Squadron, East Wretham, 16.4.41. To 12 OTU 12.6.41. FA Cat AC 11.8.41. ROS 13.8.41. ROS Vickers 17.11.41. ROS 19.12.41. To 28 OTU 7.9.42. ROS Vickers Weybridge 23.1.43. To 23 MU 22.6.43. Cat E 20.6.44.
Struck off charge 1.7.44

N2939 (ordered as NZ314)

Mark IA, Type 412 (RNZAF variant), Contract No. 781439/38
RAF serial number N2939, allocated to RNZAF
Manufactured September-October 1939, Vickers-Armstrongs, Weybridge
RNZAF order cancelled and re-directed to RAF 4.9.39

To 9 Squadron, Honington, 27.10.39. Shot down by Me110s and crashed into the sea off Wilhelmshaven with loss of all crew 18.12.39.
Struck off charge 21.2.40

N2940 (ordered as NZ315)

Mark IA, Type 412 (RNZAF variant), Contract No. 781439/38
RAF serial number N2940, allocated to RNZAF
Manufactured September-October 1939, Vickers-Armstrongs, Weybridge
RNZAF order cancelled and re-directed to RAF 4.9.39
To 9 Squadron, Honington, 27.10.39. Failed to return, probably shot down by fighter during raid on Wilhelmshaven with loss of all crew 18.12.39.

Struck off charge 21.2.40

N2941 (ordered as NZ316)

Mark IA, Type 412 (RNZAF variant), Contract No. 781439/38
RAF serial number N2941, allocated to RNZAF
Manufactured October 1939, Vickers-Armstrongs, Weybridge
RNZAF order cancelled and re-directed to RAF 4.9.39
To 9 Squadron, Honington, 27.10.39. Failed to return, probably shot down by fighter during raid on Wilhelmshaven with loss of all crew 18.12.39.
Struck off charge 21.2.40

N2942 (ordered as NZ317)

Mark IA, Type 412 (RNZAF variant), Contract No. 781439/38
Manufactured October 1939, Vickers-Armstrongs, Weybridge
RNZAF order cancelled and re-directed to RAF 4.9.39
To 9 Squadron, Honington, 5.11.39. MI Vickers 12.8.40. FA 10.10.40. To Vickers Brooklands SAS 16.10.40.
Struck off charge 21.11.40

~ ~ ~ ~ ~ ~ ~ ~

The remaining 12 Wellingtons, the fourth and fifth batches of six aircraft to be manufactured, were to have been Mark IAs, 'borrowed' from a later RAF contract. They were intended for the 3rd and 4th Mobile Flights, which were due to depart for New Zealand in July and September/October 1940 respectively.

Production blocks had yet to be allocated for RNZAF aircraft from this part of the order when it was cancelled on 4 September 1939. Their RNZAF serial numbers (NZ318–329), therefore, only ever existed on paper.

~ ~ ~ ~ ~ ~ ~ ~

Sources:

Andrew Wilson, Brooklands Museum, personal communications.

Bomber Command History Form 78 Aircraft Movement Cards, at www.lancasterbombers.net/form-78-aircraft-movement-cards-2-2/form-78-vickers-wellington/.

F/L J. Summers, Pilot's Flying Log Book, Brooklands Museum.

New Zealand contracts for Wellingtons, 1938–1951, GBR/0012/MS Vickers Doc 403, Cambridge University Library.

New Zealand Squadron Flight Authorisation Book, Air Force Museum of NZ.

No. 75 (NZ) Squadron Operations Record Book, R.A.F. Forms 540 & 541, March – May 1940, Ref: AIR/27/645/, The National Archives (UK).

Vickers Wellington – The Backbone of Bomber Command, Key Publishing, 2013.

Index

115 Squadron, 41

149 Squadron, 80, 100, 113, 121, 127

3 Group, Bomber Command, 77, 83, 91, 93, 106, 115, 124, 128

37 Squadron, 83, 111

38 Squadron, 25, 27, 37, 41, 45, 72, 73, 110, 111

75 (New Zealand) Squadron, 91, 100, 106, 110, 121, 124, 126, 127, 128, 130

75 Squadron Association, 130

9 Squadron, 41, 81

99 Squadron, 44, 71, 80, 93, 99, 100

Aachen, 116

Aarlborg, 113

Abbs, SG, 140

Adams, Gilbert, 78, 88, 104, 140

Adams, John, 43, 83, 89, 91, 101, 104, 105, 111, 112, 113, 119, 120, 140, 160

aerial honeymoon, 25

aerial photography, 23, 25, 44

Aeroplane and Armament Experimental Establishment, 71

Air Ministry specification B.9/32, 14

Airspeed Oxford, 19, 23

Air-to-Surface Vessel (ASV) radar, 35, 43, 46, 68, 69, 70

Albert, Eric, 78, 89, 140

Allen, V, 140

Allinson, William, 78, 91, 105, 140

Anderson, Ronald, 44, 73, 88, 104, 141, 160

Armstrong, Albert, 141

Arrow Aviation Company, 24

Baldwin, Air Vice-Marshal Jack, 77, 83, 93, 106, 110, 121, 124, 126, 127, 128

Barton Bendish, 71

Bassingbourn, 110, 114

Battle of Narvik, 110, 111

Bawdsey Research Station, 43

Best, Eric, 113, 129

Blazing Arrow, 24

Bloor, William, 141

bombing techniques, 120

BOMLIN, 115

Breckon, Aubrey, 42, 43, 44, 53, 72, 77, 83, 89,, 111, 113, 115, 119, 120, 130, 134, 141, 160

Bristol Blenheim, 79, 115

Brooklands, 31

Brooks, John, 78, 88, 104, 112, 116, 141

Brown, Norman, 78, 142

Buckley, Lykke 'Pat', 25, 133

Buckley, Maurice 'Buck', 16, 23, 24, 25, 27, 28, 34, 37, 41, 42, 43, 53, 67, 68, 71, 72, 73, 77, 78, 79, 82, 83, 88, 91, 93, 106, 117, 119, 121, 124, 125, 126, 128, 129, 130, 133, 142, 160

Burton, A, 142

Bussey, Benjamin, 142

Cameron, Edward, 115

camouflage scheme, first Wellingtons, 40

Campion, John, 143

Canterbury Aviation Company, 9, 24

Carter, Jim, 78, 88, 104, 124, 143

Charles, Alfred, 81, 104, 143

Clark, AE, 143

Clark, Charlie, 54, 162

Clark-Hall, Air Marshall Sir Robert, 15

Cochrane, Ralph, 10, 11, 14, 15, 16, 17, 18, 19, 21, 22, 25, 37, 70, 127, 128, 129

Cohen, Ronald, 53, 54, 72, 82, 143, 162

Colbourn, Rupert, 143, 160

Coleman, William, 43, 44, 48, 72, 74, 77, 83, 91, 101, 110, 113, 115, 119, 120, 143, 160

Collett, Wilfred, 73, 100, 106, 116, 119, 120, 121, 144

Collins, John, 43, 72, 77, 83, 88, 89, 91, 101, 104, 105, 111, 112, 115, 116, 144, 160

Colville, A, 144, 160

Cross, Ian, 37, 144

Curtis, Richard, 113, 145

Daly, Charles, 145

Daly, Group Captain APV, 41

Day, Douglas 'Reg', 78, 91, 105, 145

Dinant, 116

Dowds, John, 78, 145

Edwards, Arthur, 145

Edwards, Humphrey, 78, 146

Ellis, Robert, 78, 146

Emery, Albert, 146, 160

Fairfax, Ivan, 146

Feltwell, 83, 88, 91, 93, 100, 105, 106, 110, 111, 113, 119, 121, 124, 125, 126, 127, 130

Ferris, John, 113

Fiji, 17, 21

Findlay, James, 15, 55, 164

first wartime operation, 88, 106

Flegg, Harry, 72, 146

Flight Authorisation Book, 73, 89, 133

formation of 75 (New Zealand) Squadron, 86, 106, 121

Fowler, Philip, 24

Fraser, the Hon. Peter, 14, 69, 79, 126, 128

Freeman, Trevor, 43, 53, 83, 88, 104, 115, 120, 146, 160

French, Graham, 54, 162

Frost, Flying Officer, 72, 146

Froyennes, 116

Garrard, Sidney, 78, 147

George, Francis, 54, 162

Gethings, Sidney, 147

Gibb, John, 78, 88, 104, 147

Gibson, Esmond, 14, 15, 16, 17, 18, 21

Gilmour, Douglas, 115

Goodhue, Trevor, 54, 163

Gordon, Alexander, 147, 160

Gough, Albert, 147

Gow, Ian, 86, 147

Green, Francis, 78, 88, 104, 147

Green, Geoffrey, 148

Greenaway, Arthur, 42, 43, 68, 72, 82, 148, 160

Hamilton, Ian, 78, 148

hangars, reinforced concrete, 48, 49, 52

Hare, Maurice, 35, 36

Harkness, Donald, 79, 88, 104, 110, 111, 148

Harrington, William 'Bill', 24

Harris, Arthur, 11, 128

Harwell, 45, 72, 73, 74, 77, 78, 81, 86, 106, 126

Heligoland Bight, The Battle of, 79

Hewer, Albert, 148

Hewett, James, 26

Hobsonville, 10, 14, 16, 17, 21, 23, 25, 28, 52

Hockey, Leonard, 113, 116

Hogg, Richard, 79, 148

Hopkins, John, 37, 149

Horsfall, Geoffrey, 113

Howie, Lieutenant Commander FO, 111

Hughes, Robert, 78, 89, 110, 149

Hugill, AT, 149

Humphreys, Arthur, 113

Hunter, Charles, 42, 68, 72, 82, 149, 160

Jenkins, Thomas, 149

Jones, Bernard, 149

Jones, the Hon. Fred, 14, 15, 16, 18, 19, 54

Jonsvatnet, 113

Jordan, Bill, 93, 99, 100, 129, 130

Julian, TN, 150

Kay, Cyril 'Cyrus', 26, 27, 41, 53, 68, 77, 82, 88, 89, 93, 104, 105, 106, 111, 115, 119, 120, 121, 124, 125, 126, 127, 128, 129, 134, 150, 160

Kayll, the Reverend Arthur, 86, 119

Kingsford Smith, Charles, 25, 133

Kitson, Herbert, 78, 91, 105, 112, 150

Knight, Colin 'Tod', 80, 93, 99

Kristiansund, 113

Langridge, Jack, 93, 100

Larney, Geordie, 86, 91, 104, 150

Lucas, Albert, 151

Lucas, Fred 'Popeye', 43, 72, 74, 77, 83, 89, 91, 104, 110, 119, 120, 129, 151, 160

Ludlow-Hewitt, Air Chief Marshal Sir Edgar, 77, 93, 110

Macfarlane, Malcolm, 115

Mackay, Donald, 78, 151

MacRobertson centenary air race, 26

Mair, Geoffrey, 151

Marham, 25, 27, 29, 37, 41, 43, 48, 53, 55, 68, 71, 72, 78, 93, 121

Marsden, Dr Ernest, 35, 43, 46, 53, 68, 69

Martlesham Heath, 25

Martyn, Dr David, 46

Mathews, HR, 152

McArthur, Duncan, 115

McGlashan, Donald, 44, 68, 73, 86, 152, 161

McKee, Andrew, 80, 93

Mead, Thomas, 152

Mees, H, 72, 152, 161

Methwold, 83

Meyer-Williams, Pilot Officer, 45, 152

Mifflin, Joseph, 152

Miller, Malcolm, 115

Mitchell, William, 121

Mobile Flight, 41, 48, 53, 54, 55, 68, 71, 72, 78, 93, 160, 162

Modin, Group Captain Charles, 93, 100

Morrison, Ian, 53, 54, 72, 82, 152, 162

Mumby, Thomas, 83, 89, 110, 111, 153

Murphy, John, 78, 153

Murphy, Patrick 'Spud', 153

Murray, Norman, 54, 163

Narvik, 110, 111

Nash, the Hon. Walter, 14, 43, 46

Nevill, Arthur, 14, 16

Nevill, William, 83, 88, 153

New Zealand Aero Transport Company, 23

New Zealand Flight, 77, 78, 86, 106, 121

New Zealand Liaison Officer (NZLO) to the Air Ministry, 27, 28, 77, 156

New Zealand Squadron, 41, 53, 54, 55, 71, 77, 78, 79, 83, 86, 88, 93, 133, 140

Newell, Squadron Leader Fred, Assistant Liaison Officer, 82, 93, 126

nickeling, 104, 105, 106, 110

No.1 Squadron RNZAF, 48

No.2 Squadron RNZAF, 52

NZ Permanent Air Force (NZPAF), 9, 10, 25, 28

Ohakea, 7, 8, 16, 17, 19, 21, 48, 52, 113, 125, 128, 129

Parker, PS, 153, 161

Pearce, Leslie, 153, 161

Permanent Flight, 41

Perrott, George, 54, 163

Pettit, Squadron Leader, 72, 153

Pimbley, George, 154

Piper, Harold, 26

Pomeroy, W, 72, 154, 161

Portal, Air Chief Marshal Charles, 11, 117, 124, 127

Powell, Group Captain John 'Speedy', 127

Pownall, Charles, 113, 116

radar development in New Zealand, 35, 46, 69

Radio Direction Finding (RDF), 35, 43, 46, 69

RAF Staff College, 11, 28

Rafferty, Edward, 154

Read, Frank, 78, 154

Read, Thomas 'Dick', 41, 73, 121, 154, 161

Renshaw, John, 154, 161

Rhodes, Alan, 154

'rhubarb', 115

Rider, William, 154, 161

Roberts, Edwin, 41, 73, 121, 154

Rock, William, 155

Rongotai, 19, 129

Rose-Price, Arthur, 37, 155

Ross, Benjamin, 155

Royal Naval Air Service (RNAS), 10, 15, 23, 24

Royal New Zealand Air Force (RNZAF), 7, 10, 14, 15, 16, 18, 19, 22, 23, 25, 27, 31, 34, 35, 37, 41, 43, 48, 53, 54, 55, 69, 71, 77, 81, 82, 86, 93, 100, 116, 125, 127, 128, 129, 130

Sach, Sergeant, 45, 155

Samoan Clipper, 17, 25

Sawrey-Cookson, Wing Commander Reginald, 127

Schilling Roads, 93

Shuttleworth, Bernard, 78, 155

Silloth, 83, 114

Singapore, 9, 10, 11, 15, 17, 23, 69

Skinner, SR, Chief Clerk, New Zealand House, 93

Smith, Harold, 78, 155

Smith, Richard 'Dick', 73, 155

Smith, Thomas, 54, 163

Sockburn (see Wigram), 9, 24

Southern Alps, first flight across, 24

Southern Cross, 25, 133

Sparling, Frank De Labouchere-, 113, 116

Special Sweep, 88, 89, 91, 106, 110

Stavanger, 100, 112, 115

Steven, William 'Bill', 41, 73, 121, 156, 161

Stewart, Frank, 26

Stradishall, 83, 124, 126

Summers, Joseph 'Mutt', 25, 35, 36, 71

Swetman, John, 156, 161

Tainui, 26

Taphouse, Henry, 156

Taylor, Frank, 156

Thomas, Eric, 156

Thorpe, George, 78, 88, 104, 116, 156

Tournai, 116

Trondheim, 111, 113

Turner, Charles, 48

Turrell, Ernest, 156

Ulm, Charles, 25, 133

Værnes, 111, 113

Vickers gun turrets, 35, 73, 81

Vickers Type 271, 14

Vickers Type 403, 34, 165

Vickers Vildebeest, 10, 25, 69, 113

Vickers Wellesley, 14, 34

Vickers Wellington, 15, 17, 18, 19, 23, 25, 31

Vickers Wellington Mark I, 25, 31, 35, 36, 44, 71, 73, 83, 165

Vickers Wellington Mark IA, 35, 36, 53, 71, 83, 167, 169

Vickers Wellington Mark IC, 114

Vickers, Vickers-Armstrongs Limited, 10, 14, 25, 31, 34, 35, 36, 55, 68

Waalhaven, 115

Wallingford, Sidney, 27, 28, 31, 35, 37, 41, 42, 53, 55, 67, 68, 71, 77, 78, 93, 129, 156, 163

Wallis, Barnes, 10, 14, 15, 34, 128

Watson, Samuel, 79, 157

Weybridge, 31, 35, 37, 42, 71, 83

Whenuapai, 17, 19, 52, 129

White, Jack, 157, 161

White, Joseph 'Joe', 44, 73, 86, 157, 161

White, Lewis, 78, 157

Wick, 110, 111, 113

Wigram, 9, 15, 17, 19, 21, 24, 25, 27, 42, 43, 52, 54, 55, 93, 113, 128, 133

Wigram, Sir Henry, 9

Wilhelmshaven, 80

Wilkes, Tom, 10, 14, 15

Williams, Edwin 'Ted', 44, 73, 89, 110, 111, 113, 124, 158, 161

Williams, Neville, 43, 77, 83, 91, 101, 110, 112, 115, 119, 120, 158, 161

Williams, Wilfred 'Bill', 43, 68, 83, 91, 110, 111, 113, 115, 158, 161

Yates, Arthur, 159

www.ingramcontent.com/pod-product-compliance
Lightning Source LLC
Chambersburg PA
CBHW062130160426
43191CB00013B/2253